Sunderland
MEMORIES

The publishers would like to thank the following companies for their

support in the production of this book

City of Sunderland College

George V Cumming

John G Hogg

H Nordstrom & Son

Sunderland High School

Edward Thompson

Town Centre Cars

Fred Williamson & Sons

Willowcrete Manufacturing Company Limited

First published in Great Britain by True North Books Limited
England HX3 6AE
01422 344344

ISBN 1 903204 95 X

Text, design and origination by True North Books
Printed and bound by The Amadeus Press

Sunderland MEMORIES

CONTENTS

INTRODUCTION

Here is an opportunity to take a walk down memory lane, turn into nostalgia park and stroll along yesteryear road. 'Sunderland Memories' is the latest in the series of True North books that take a look back into the last century and help us recall just how things used to be in our city before bombing raids and town planners changed its face. This book is an opportunity to wander down Fawcett Street and shop at Binns once again or drive a Ford Prefect along Holmeside without any restrictions. All the photographs within have been enhanced by the attachment of captions intended to inform or even provoke comment. They are not image titles but text designed to highlight elements of each photograph and, on occasion, offer a pithy outlook on the background or times in which the scenes were observed. Hopefully, this will prompt the reader into reflecting on his or her own interpretation. Feel free to disagree, for then we have succeeded in stimulating discussion. That can only be of benefit as we think back over how life might have been in the times depicted or how it really was if we are old enough to recall those days. Perhaps for some of us those memories have a hazy hue and the photographs will help bring everything flooding back. The camera never lies, though its angles might offer a slightly different perspective.

This collection of delightful photographs brings back to life a time when attitudes and society in general were so different. There really was an age when mobile phones did not disturb the peace of the lounge bar in the pub. Men offered their seats to women on the bus or touched their hats in the streets when wishing a lady a good morning. Children called their teachers 'sir' and 'miss' and never realised that the adults lecturing them had an existence outside the schoolroom. Supermarkets and shopping malls, ugly concrete office blocks and super fast highways and ring roads were still to come when many of these images were captured. The book makes no apology for indulging in that warm glow of reflecting on the past. Times have changed, not always for the better, however not everything new is to be dismissed as a lowering of standards. 'Sunderland Memories' will also remind the reader of wartime days, when we feared the worst as bombers flew overhead on missions to smash our shipyards and cow the city's citizens, but it is with the aggressive intentions of invaders other than the Nazis that the real history of the city begins.

There is only modest evidence of Roman involvement in the area, so it is with the Anglo Saxons that we must first look for signs of our city heritage. In 674 A.D the land on the northern bank of the river overlooking the coast at Wearmouth was granted by Ecgfrith, King of Northumbria, to the nobleman, Benedict Biscop. He used the land to build a monastery on the site that was later used by the church of St Peter. However, warmongering Vikings and Scots both sacked the monastery and

Sunderland remained a small coastal settlement for many centuries. Its growth as a coal exporter was restricted by fierce opposition from Newcastle, a town that possessed a Royal Charter and resisted the attempts of its neighbours in trying to rival the Tyneside supremacy. During the English Civil War of the mid 17th century, Sunderland threw its support behind the Parliamentarians under Cromwell, thus thumbing its nose at the Royalist Newcastle and Durham. One major result of this was that Sunderland and its coal trade began to expand rapidly after the war while Newcastle, though remaining the major coal port of Britain, had permanently lost its virtual monopoly on the export of local coal.

Shipbuilding was one of the main sources of economic stability for the area from as far back as medieval times. The town, though, still suffered from an identity crisis. Sunderland was only a part of Wearmouth and although the name was commonly used for the whole area, it was not until 1719 that Sunderland itself achieved the status of a separate parish. It was not until 1897 that the roles were finally reversed and Monkwearmouth officially became part of the town of Sunderland. By then, during the 19th century Sunderland's number of shipyards had grown from 24 in 1814 to 65 in 1840. By the mid twentieth century, when the town produced more than a quarter of the nation's total tonnage of merchant and naval ships for World War II, Sunderland was widely regarded as the largest shipbuilding town in the world. It did not achieve city status, of course, until 1992.

The town's great expansion took place during the 1800s thanks to these two major industries that flourished as the industrial revolution changed the face of Britain from an agricultural economy to one based on smoke and grime. So rapid was the change that it magnified the gulf between the working and middle classes. Wealthier groups moved out of the old Sunderland port area, leaving less advantaged residents behind who were also faced with an influx from the rural areas as people moved off the land and into towns in search of work. This led to overcrowding and the inevitable spread of disease amongst those in the squalid living conditions. An outbreak of cholera in 1831 coincided with the beginning of modern urban local government with the first elected borough corporation. This helped considerably in the move towards civic improvement, although deprivation and mortality rates remained high. By the 20th century the main pattern of modern Sunderland had been established, with the three main communities in Bishopwearmouth, Sunderland and Monkwearmouth. Other outlying communities such as Grangetown and Fulwell began to be absorbed, along with the resorts of Roker and Seaburn that grew in popularity because of the rise of the local holiday and excursion industries that served visitors from as far away as Scotland until the 1950s and the overseas package travel deals took over.

But, times change and progress marches ever steadily on. The shipyards lie idle and the coalfields remain quiet. Instead, we have had to turn to car manufacturers from overseas and service industries to underpin our modern economy. We have

to look to the future, but there comes a time when it is pleasant to take a backward glance and recall those days when times were different. We shall leave it up to the individual reader to decide whether or not they were any better.

You are now nearly ready to turn the first page and bring back memories of the city near where Lewis Carroll was inspired to write 'The Walrus and the Carpenter'. That fine 19th century novelist and poet used his imagination to give us his Alice stories. Now use yours to turn the looking glass on elegant buildings, jaunty shop awnings and people who talked of shillings and pence, quarts and gills, furlongs and yards. Put a stack of Film Fun comics and Famous Five books by your side to heighten the experience. Turn on the wireless for 'Workers' Playtime' or place on the gramophone a 78 record of Nat 'King' Cole singing 'Unforgettable'. With a glass of cream soda in one hand, a Kensitas cigarette dangling from the fingers of the other and a bag of misshapes from the sweetie shop on your knee, it is time to go begin. Become an Ovaltiney once more or pin on that Robertson's golly badge. Get in the mood and let 'Sunderland Memories' bring it all flooding back.

Sunderland has much to be proud of and a number of its best known and longest established firms have allowed us to access their internal archives. This has enabled us to recount the history of these companies from humble beginnings, in most cases, to leading positions in their chosen area of expertise. These organisations have tremendous social, as well as commercial significance, as between them they represent the places of employment for many thousands of Sunderland people. We are very grateful to the directors of these businesses for their co-operation and valuable support. Let the nostalgia begin.

Left: This must have been the sort of view that a bomb aimer had of our city when the Luftwaffe flew overhead during the last war. The aeroplane from which this photograph was taken did not have to worry about being picked out by searchlights or having to dodge the flak sent its way from the ack ack guns trained upon it. Those of us born in the second half of the last century cannot truly appreciate what it must have been like for both the Germans and the pilots of the RAF as they flew over large areas of population on a their bombing raids. We can use our imagination and read through the archives to get some sense of what it was like to be on the ground as the payload was delivered from the skies, but there has been only a limited amount written about the feelings of those who flew above. We know that they were anxious and, at times, frightened as fighter planes hunted them down and anti aircraft shells burst around them, but we know little of what they felt as they pulled the levers that sent 1,000 pounds of high explosive spiralling down to the ground. Did they give consideration to the people far below who might be blown to smithereens, or was it something that they could black out of their minds?

STREET SCENES

The Durham and Sunderland Railway Company brought the first passenger services to the town in 1836. The line came in from the south, along the coast to South Dock where the terminus was known as Town Moor. This was replaced by Hendon Station in 1858 at a point where the line had to be joined by the Newcastle and Darlington Junction Railway line to Penshaw and Durham. Central Station was originally known as New Station and had a single entrance and street level buildings at the North End, but a second entrance and associated buildings at the south were added five years later. This view of the arched entrance at South End was taken in 1938 and there were already plans afoot for a new station to be built. The onset of war delayed matters, as did a bombing raid n 1943 that badly damaged the structure. It was not until 1953 that a new roof was completed, along with some other refurbishments. A complete rebuilding was undertaken in 1964 and completed the following year. It was remodelled again at the start of this century to accommodate Metro services. When Central Station was photographed, Britain's locomotives were enjoying one of the golden ages of steam. Speed records were set during the mid 1930s on a regular basis, culminating in the magnificent 126 mph achieved by the Mallard in July 1938.

Above and right: The Empire Theatre was a partnership between Edward Moss, Oswald Stoll and local man Richard Thornton. The Empire is the North East's largest theatre and a splendid example of Edwardian architecture. It has a 90ft round tower crowned with a dome and a revolving sphere which bore the statue of "Terpsichore" the Greek Goddess of dance.

Some of the top names in entertainment have appeared at the Empire, these include, Charlie Chaplin, Laurel & Hardy, George Formby and The Beatles. Theatre attendance was low in the 1950s due to the advent of television and cinemascope, so it closed in May 1959. Sunderland Corporation took the unprecedented step of buying the theatre and it became the first theatre under civic control in the UK. Since reopening in 1960 the theatre has had several refurbishments. After the latest 4.5 million refurbishment in 2005, the Empire now boasts 21st century facilities and is the only theatre between Manchester and Edinburgh capable of staging large West End productions.

Right: A sign in the window says that horsehair is bought here, but for what purpose we can only hazard a guess. There are also some horse brasses to be seen through the window to the right. What we do know is that this natural material was used for weaving with a cotton warp in about 1800 by cottage industries. The horsehair fabrics were initially woven by hand. This would require a weaver to stand at a loom all day and a small child would sit in the loom with the horse tail, serving the hair to the weaver. The Education Act of 1870, ensuring that all children went to school, led to the development of mechanical looms that could tease one hair from a tail. Horsehair has had many other uses, including being turned into jewellery, for the bristles on brushes, violin bows and for stuffing furniture. The craftsman in the picture had some examples of his work displayed above his head and was demonstrating his art to a fascinated group of children. Such instances of traditional craft are generally only seen these days at country fairs or open air museums that are dedicated to the way that we used to live. Such examples of living history reinforce the lesson much more interestingly and forcefully than any dry description in a schoolroom text book.

Left: Once upon a time, little girls looked like little girls, all sugar and spice and all things nice. This angelic tot would have been the apple of her father's eye and perhaps grew up to break a few lads' hearts in the 1950s. If things went to plan, she might have married, raised her own family and now be sitting by the fireside in her old age, thumbing through this book and thinking back to the days when she played with her dolls in the parlour and enjoyed hopscotch on the pavement. She was on Fighting Cock Lane in c1935. It does not take Hercule Poirot to determine the so called sporting activity that once flourished in this vicinity. The pretty subject of this photograph seems out of place here as this lane was an infamous slum, notorious for immorality and violence. Situated on the north side of High Street East near the Grey Horse pub, Fighting Cock Lane was once known as Holmes Lane and, in the 18th century, had a mixture of cottages and light industry that included printing, wood turning and pipe making. The cottages were pulled down in the mid 1930s and the lane was eventually closed and itself demolished in April 1955.

Above: Oh dear. Like some rhino brought down by the high powered rifle of a white hunter, this noble tram lay wounded. Broken glass and metal shards were scattered across Hylton Road and sparks flew from the overhead cables as the pantograph electric collector left its mounting. But this beast was not mown down by a .303 bullet. The damage had been done by a brewer's lorry carelessly reversing into the road beside the Mountain Dairy. The Circle No 70 tram, coming down from Millfield Station, toppled with all the grace it could muster, but nothing could prevent the force of gravity that ensured its finishing position on its side. Some of the windows were smashed by rescuers who rushed to help the dazed passengers who must have wondered what hit them. Fortunately, no one was seriously injured, but 13 still required hospital treatment for cuts, bruising and shock. The accident happened on 15th June 1933 and collected quite a crowd of onlookers.

Right: In Victorian times it was quite common for a couple to have as many as six or eight children. A sad comment on the living conditions of the time is that infant mortality was high, as any visit to a churchyard will reveal. Consequently, those large families were depleted by the time that the surviving children reached adulthood. In 1900, the average life expectancy of an infant was just 45. By the time of this post World War I photograph, advances in medicine and sanitation meant that children had a better chance of reaching maturity than ever before. This had an economic effect on the poor, however, as they still produced large families, but had more surviving mouths to feed. Many could not escape from their existence on the breadline. Stone Yard Low Quay was home to these people, but it was an area where they found survival difficult. Work was not plentiful in the 1920s and a number of the women living here had been widowed in the war. It was a tough existence for the lower end of society. The whitewashed entry led up a flight of steps to Stone Yard, but these homes are no more. They were demolished in the 1930s to make way for the new Corporation Quay.

Left: Never were eyes in the back of his head more needed by anyone than in the case of the policeman on point duty on Holmeside, where it meets Crowtree Road and Park Lane, for he was in dire danger of being flattened by the oncoming tram approaching from Borough Road, to the east. Presumably, his ears alerted him in time because the clanking tram was not the quietest of vehicles on our roads in those days, though the rattle of Magog's removal van would have provided some cover if the tram driver had an evil streak to his nature! Today, to the left we can find Debenham's and an entrance to the Bridges Shopping Centre

The trams in front of the Town Hall on Fawcett Street are perfect for giving this photograph a period feel as they belong to an age in the first half of the last century when the traffic on our roads was so different. There were fewer cars, no one way streets and nothing in the form of traffic calming measures or pedestrianisation. The No 56 tram gave good service. Supplied in 1908, it had been rebuilt in 1926. All the public service vehicles pictured carried adverts for Binns, the department store that they were just about to pass, below the Town Hall. George Binns, a Quaker, opened a small draper's shop on High Street in 1783. He moved from this spot, opposite the old market cross near George Street, to other premises on High Street. The slogan 'Shop at Binns' could be seen on every Sunderland tram from 1924 onwards. Not a bad bit of adverting business, as it cost the company just 10 shillings (50p) per tram.

Right: Situated in Marsden Bay on one of the most attractive stretches of the north east coastline, this grotto is well known for its sea bird colonies, with pairs of kittiwakes, fulmars and gulls. Marsden Rock was one of the superb views in the vicinity, but its face was changed forever when the famous arch collapsed in 1996. The cove was a smugglers' haven in earlier times and steps run all the way from the top of the cliff down to the shore. The Marsden Grotto public house, seen in 1948, is a hostelry with a long history. In 1782, an Allendale lead miner nicknamed 'Jack the Blaster' came to work in the nearby limestone quarries and also became the grotto's first permanent occupant, setting up home with his wife here. This naturally created cave became a favourite haunt of the smugglers who worked along this stretch of coast. As his nickname suggests, he is said to have enlarged the cave with explosives and probably also built the steps that climb to the north. From his grotto home he dispensed refreshments to smugglers and to the growing number of more public visitors to the bay. In 1828, Peter Allan, then publican of the Jolly Sailor Inn at Whitburn, succeeded Jack and continued his work by excavating further rooms out of the solid rock. In 1891 the Vaux brewery acquired the lease and helped it develop into a popular and successful establishment, buying it outright in 1938.

Left: Work took place in October 1938 at the North End of Central Station as workmen dug the foundations for a group of kiosks that were to be built in front of the portico. Little did they know at the time that five years later the Luftwaffe would come to call and destroy much of the station and parts of the surrounding areas. Some should have realised what the future held because, just as they sank their shovels into the ground, the newspapers that these men had read that morning were full of the German invasion of Czechoslovakia. This made Prime Minister Chamberlain a laughing stock as he had come back from a meeting with the German Chancellor the month before declaring that he had secured 'peace in our time' with a written promise from Hitler. There was revolution in the air within government ranks. The First Lord of the Admiralty resigned and several; prominent Tories openly criticised their leader. Chamberlain narrowly survived a vote of confidence, but the knives were already being sharpened, though it would be another 18 months before Churchill took over at the helm. By then, trains in and out of Central Station were carrying troops and transporting materials to help in the war effort and some of the labourers in the photograph had been called up for active service.

Above: It was April 1954 and Binns' famous department store dominated the left hand side of Fawcett Street, as viewed from Gas Office Corner. The Northern Gas Board showroom abutted that of the firm that was synonymous with good taste in all household requirements. Binns also had premises on the opposite side of the road and attracted the general public from far and wide. Rationing had finally come to an end and we were free to spend our money as and how we liked, at long last. That was if we had any to spare as the austerity of the immediate postwar years was not completely dead and buried just yet. One of the last trams that we would see trundled towards the junction with Borough Road where the cameraman stood with his back to Mowbray Gardens. The new Museum and Winter Gardens now occupy the right hand corner of this spot, just off camera. Wilkinson's has replaced the name of Binns on the left, while the new library, gallery and Connexions are on the right these days. Another change, and not for the better, saw the demolition of the Town Hall. Its grandeur was lost to the city over 35 years ago and now we have the Northern Rock building and entrance area to the Bridges Shopping Centre in its stead.

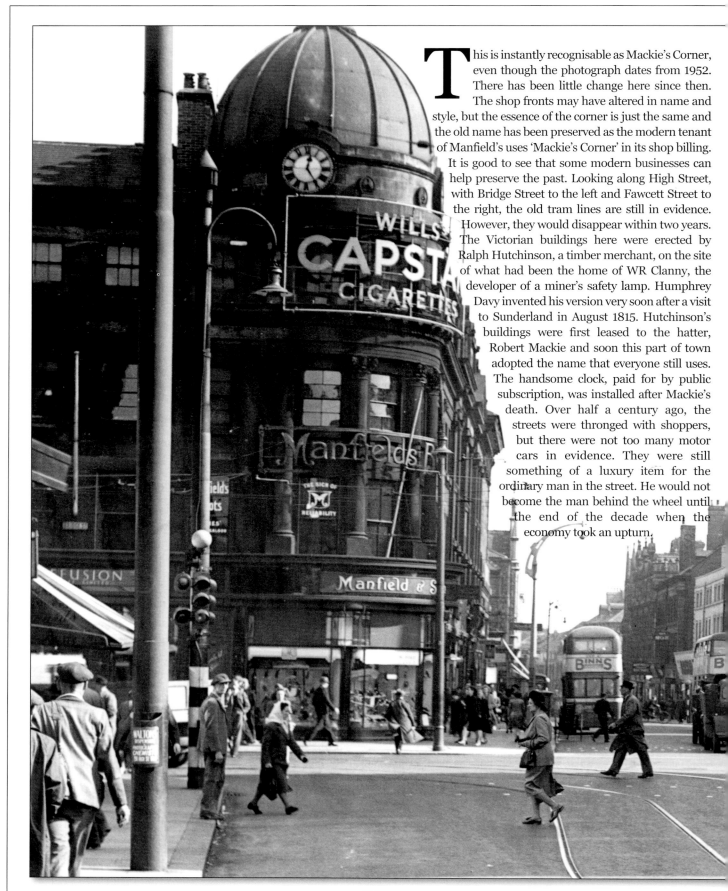

This is instantly recognisable as Mackie's Corner, even though the photograph dates from 1952. There has been little change here since then. The shop fronts may have altered in name and style, but the essence of the corner is just the same and the old name has been preserved as the modern tenant of Manfield's uses 'Mackie's Corner' in its shop billing. It is good to see that some modern businesses can help preserve the past. Looking along High Street, with Bridge Street to the left and Fawcett Street to the right, the old tram lines are still in evidence. However, they would disappear within two years. The Victorian buildings here were erected by Ralph Hutchinson, a timber merchant, on the site of what had been the home of WR Clanny, the developer of a miner's safety lamp. Humphrey Davy invented his version very soon after a visit to Sunderland in August 1815. Hutchinson's buildings were first leased to the hatter, Robert Mackie and soon this part of town adopted the name that everyone still uses. The handsome clock, paid for by public subscription, was installed after Mackie's death. Over half a century ago, the streets were thronged with shoppers, but there were not too many motor cars in evidence. They were still something of a luxury item for the ordinary man in the street. He would not become the man behind the wheel until the end of the decade when the economy took an upturn.

Above: Wearmouth Miners' Hall is just visible in this 1970 photograph and, at the time, was a flourishing centre for those employed in the industry that had provided Sunderland with one of its economic cornerstones for several centuries. Wearmouth Colliery stood where the Stadium of Light now hosts the city's soccer supporters and was the last of the former County Durham coalfields to close when it ceased production in 1994. At its peak, just after the first world war, there were 173,000 miners at work across the county. Production fell after the last war as demand for coal slipped and the industry went into terminal decline. A monument to the Davy lamp stands outside the football ground as a reminder of the past. The photograph is dominated by The Lighthouse on Roker Avenue at Wheatsheaf Corner, as seen from North Bridge Street. This distinctive building was destroyed in a fire in 1971. The Wheatsheaf public house is on the opposite corner.

Above: Standing in a prominent position on the corner of Holmeside, Vine Place and Brougham Street, the ABC Cinema was screening 'Serpico', a rather gloomy and violent 1973 movie about police corruption. Starring Al Pacino, the film was well received by cinema audiences and spawned a spin off television series a few years later. The ABC finished its time as the Cannon in 1999, having first come to our notice as the Ritz in 1937 when it opened its doors on 1st March with a screening of 'Swing Time' with Fred Astaire and Ginger Rogers. Going to the pictures, as it was known, was one of the main attractions of the week either side of the last war. You certainly got your money's worth. There were usually two films to be seen, along with a newsreel, a cartoon and an informative short. If that was not enough, then you could always take a sly look at what Doris and Arthur were getting up to on the back row until that spoilsport of an usherette shone her torch on them. Back in the early 20th century, Sunderland had as many as 23 outlets showing films, including converted chapels and halls as well as purpose built picture houses. The first ever showing in the town of a moving picture took place in Toward Road at the Victoria Hall. The visiting Tussaud's Exhibition gave locals such gripping stuff as 'An Operation in a Dentist's Chair' and 'Blacksmiths at Work in a Forge'. The cinema is now known as The Point, housing the Arizona Purple Bar and Union Velvet Lounge.

Right: Members of the Thistle Club dressed up warmly on this January day in 1978 as they looked forward to a belated Christmas treat at the Odeon on Holmeside. There were several films billed on the hoardings as current features or future events, but we are not certain which, if any, provided the entertainment for this happy bunch. 'The Pink Panther Strikes Again' with the hilarious Peter Sellers or 'The Deep', a thriller based on a Peter Benchley book, may not have been the choice. 'Star Wars' was a possibility as it certainly broke some box office records during its run. Whatever the offering, it probably fell into the category of 'family entertainment'. This was something that these children's parents did not recall from their younger days as then there were special showings just for that age group. Saturday matinees were part of their way of life. Instead of being smothered in an over protective cocoon, in the postwar era of the 1950s youngsters were allowed to go out on their own or with pals from their age group. Cinemas showed cartoons, a cowboy film with Hopalong Cassidy, comedy shorts with the Three Stooges and serials with Flash Gordon. Those weekly episodes of stirring deeds were especially popular as the hero was always left in a cliffhanging situation. Formerly the Regal, this cinema opened in 1932 and closed in 1982.

6,000 PACKETS OF SWEETS A WEEK !

Yes children that is what it costs your town — every week — to repair the damage that is caused by vandals. Silly isn't it? We all have to pay for it, and that means less for us all.

BE WISE · DON'T VANDALISE ST

A message from Councillor Gerry Graham, Chairman of South Tyneside Town Development Committee

THIS BUS SHELTER WINDOW COSTS £65 TO REPLACE

we all have to pay for vandalism!

Left and above: Vandalism and criminal damage costs a packet. This was the basis of the message put out by Councillor Gerry Graham, Chairman of the South Tyneside Town Development Committee. The sticker was pasted onto bus shelters across the area and attempted to bring home to vandals the reality of the expense involved in repairing the damage they had caused. The other idea was to make youngsters translate the cost into something that they might understand by expressing it in bags of sweets.

AT LEISURE

Looking across the beach at Roker, we can see Holey Rock, so named by locals because the promontory is riddled with holes and caverns. In the past, it was customary to keep pieces of the rock as charms. Holey Rock features a unique formation of concretionary limestone nicknamed 'cannonball rocks', found nowhere else in the world. In 1937, much of it was blown up by the local authority because it had become unstable and was crumbling. There was a real concern that a major accident was just waiting to happen. Paddling in the sea here was a most enjoyable pastime for those enjoying a day on the sands in the early 1900s.

Swimming, though, was only in its infancy as a popular recreation and social attitudes towards mixed bathing were still very conservative. Women, in particular, wore heavy costumes that covered much of their bodies and were not particularly conducive towards developing a mastery of the waters. So, for many, it was a stroll along the promenade and a happy lifting of the skirts to reveal a neatly turned ankle as they risked their toes in the briny. Cheeky little lads had less inhibition. They rushed in and out of the shallows, kicking salt water all over their big sisters who squealed with mock terror in the way that big sisters always do.

Above: Taken outside the Winter Gardens in c1930, this collection of smartly dressed people was about to take part in a staff outing. Although we do not know for certain, it is likely to be a good guess if we say that the bowler hatted men in the middle of the front row were managerial class. Just like any soccer team photo, the captain always took up that position. They are also the only two males sporting any form of headgear and the nature of their choice marks them out as important figures. The younger of the pair seems to be quite a dapper chappie, with his three piece suit and the watch chain adorning his waistcoat pocket. No doubt, some of the younger females on the staff thought that he would have been quite a catch, but they were likely to have wished in vain. He might humour them with a smile, but his leaning was more probably towards some daughter of a middle class family who stayed at home practising her needlecraft as she waited for Mr Right to come along. Those in the photograph who were looking for a husband would have been better advised to aim their sights at one of the clerks or office staff. The style of collar and tie chosen by the more mature man, seated in the centre, seems quite old fashioned in what must have been about 1930, if the women's hats are any clue.

Above right: Sponsored and partly financed by Rowland Burdon MP, Wearmouth Bridge enabled the axis of the town to turn to a north-south route along Bridge Street and Fawcett Street. The bridge had to span the river without a central arch as the bed was unsuitable in not permitting a firm foundation to be laid. Stone was too expensive and wood too shortlived, so the example of the 1779 iron bridge at Coalbrookdale was copied. This copy of a lottery ticket is of one that was issued to raise funds for the upkeep of the bridge. The prize was a share in the toll money paid to cross the bridge or the rights to ferry people across the river. Such private lotteries were created by

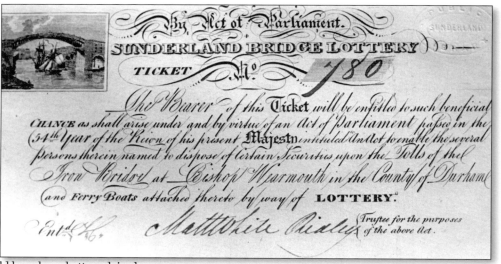

Acts of Parliament and were regulated by the Lottery Office. Numbered tickets in lotteries were sold to people for as much as £10 each, the equivalent to £500 in today's money, so it was hardly a flutter available to the man in the street. Although this ticket is undated, amateur detectives will be able to use clues in the text. It refers to 'the 54th year of the reign of his present Majesty'. As that must be George III, it puts us into 1815. However, this is a slight anomaly as records tell us that the draw took place on 31 October 1816.

Below right: Oh I do like to be beside the seaside. Little modesty huts for changing into your dippers, deck chairs that threatened to amputate the fingers of the unwary as they unfolded them and hardly a spare spot on the beach for anyone to play cricket was the way it was during a sunny day at Seaburn in the 1940s and 1950s. We took our holidays at home or just went a bit further along the coast. Foreign travel was going as far as Anglesey or the Isle of Man, but who wanted to go there when there were the glorious beaches of the north east on our doorstep? One of the most wonderful of summers occurred in 1947 and how we needed some sun on our backs. The winter had been appalling, with the country freezing its way to a standstill as the cold weather caused power cuts and led to food supplies becoming stranded in railway sidings as the tracks froze. Even the thaw brought problems with extensive flooding and just when we thought it could not get any worse, rationing was made even more restrictive. At least the sun came out and cheered us up a bit. We did not know or care about sun block and factor this, that and the other. We knotted the corners of our hankies, stuck them onto our heads and snoozed happily as the kids buried us in sand.

Below: The young women and girls were enjoying the fun of Seaham Camp in 1938. This was an extremely popular way of spending a short holiday and contributed to by school groups, guides, scouts and other similar organisations. Getting out into the fresh air was both encouraged and enjoyed by everyone who participated. Many were able to escape the smoky towns and cities and be invigorated by sea breezes and the freedom of getting back to nature, at least in part. Such activities for both sexes were thought to be character building as well, making young people both self reliant and, yet, able to work as part of a team. Such comradeship would soon be tested to the full. Already, the storm clouds were gathering over Europe. This summer would be the last full one we could enjoy in peace. Despite Mr Chamberlain's visit to Munich and the promise he wrung from Hitler, most realists knew that the little piece of paper the Prime Minister flourished contained hollow assurances. By the summer of 1939 these campers were practising air raid drills and checking their gas masks, so no one was completely surprised when the radio broadcast news that war had broken out on that fateful first Sunday in September. For many, camps would become army camps and not places of fun and happiness.

Below: Sunderland's iron bridge helped change the face of the town when it opened towards the end of the 18th century. No longer was there a need for overcrowded ferry boats at this point, such as the one that foundered in 1795, drowning 17 passengers. However, further upstream, if you just wanted to pop across the water from North to South Hylton, for example, then it was a bit of a hike to go down to the bridge and back up again on the other side. Nowadays, most of us have cars, so the journey only takes a few minutes, but in 1941 such transport was largely confined to the middle classes. In addition, there was a war on and petrol was strictly rationed. The ferry at Cox Green saved a lot of shoe leather. For just a few coppers, this family could travel quite serenely as the ferryman sat on his thwart and pulled them across. Sometimes, those who had stayed at the Oddfellows Arms a little too long were glad that they could have safe passage across the river. Perhaps it was a sight like this that inspired Josh McCrae to sing 'Messing about on the river', though for the man at the oars this was hard work.

Above: A frozen lake in Roker Park made a good skating rink for this group of lads enjoying themselves in 1958. They had no need of special boots, just ordinary shoes or wellies sufficed. These were part of the baby boomer brigade, born in the immediate postwar years when the birthrate went through the roof. While hostilities were upon them, many couples delayed starting a family as they were not sure what sort of a world it would be into which they would bring a child. For others, it was a case of lack of opportunity. Men were away at the front or confined in prison camps, so the chance of adding to the family numbers did not present itself until they returned. When they did, nature took its course and the stork put in for overtime. These boys will be getting their first bus passes about now, but we bet that they can recall those great days of their childhood when they played conkers, made soapbox carts, fired catapults and climbed trees. They kicked an old tennis ball around the streets in an after school game of 20 a side football or got an old bat, impregnated with linseed oil, out of the shed and pretended to be Denis Compton. No boy of the boomer years was ever bored or felt that he had nothing to do. If there was nothing on offer he made his own entertainment.

Below: It has not been all shipyards, docks and heavy engineering on Wearside over the years. There has been time to take to the waters in lighter pursuits, as in this example from the Roker Regatta in 1971. Today, such keen sailors as Phil Murray, Roger Bacon and Phil Lingwood can be seen participating in the inshore event that has become as annual fixture in the sporting calendar. The event, now some 100 years old, is organised by the Regatta Committee as a joint venture between the Wear Boating Association and the Sunderland Yacht Club. Situated near the Old North Pier, overlooking the harbour, the Yacht Club was formed in 1935. However, its origins go back much further, having its roots in the Royal Wear Yacht Club that was well patronised in the 19th century. A new clubhouse was built to coincide with the reformation in 1935, but this was handed over to the Sea Scouts after the war and a new wooden building was erected in 1946. The club relocated in 1957 and again in the 1990s to its present position. The Wear Boating Association acts as a co-ordinator of most events and activities involving all types of craft. As an island nation, it is not surprising that we enjoy our sailing boats. Formal events, such as our own regatta, attract healthy numbers of competitors and spectators alike. Cowes and Henley have their supporters, but the Roker Regatta is not far behind in its level of prestige.

Left: Seaburn was one of the artist LS Lowry's favourite places. His connection with the area is remembered by a large replica of one of his paintings that greets shoppers visiting Morrison's supermarket that was built in the late 1980s when the old funfair was redeveloped. This part of the coast was immensely popular with holidaymakers in the first half of the last century. Day tripping here by foot or rail took place in Victorian times, but developed into a major industry after the building of a promenade, pier and bathing huts at Roker around the turn of the century. The promenade was extended to Seaburn in the 1920s and the funfair we see here was built before the last war as workers won the right to take a paid holiday. The helter skelter, fairground rides and sideshows were well patronised. Illuminations lit up the sea front for the first time in 1937 and, although they were stopped after 1959, they were revived in the 1980s. The big dipper that opened on 28 May 1955 became the funfair's most popular ride, even if it does look a little tame in comparison with modern thrill giving contraptions. It towered 100 feet above the ground and cost £75,000 to build its 1.25 mile long track. More timid souls limited themselves to a ride on the miniature railway at the front of the funfair.

Below: An elephant ride was a popular feature in zoos and large amusement parks at one time, before the politically correct lobby decided that this was cruel and demeaning for this great beast. That the animal would have dragged tree trunks large distances at some logging plant in its own home country and been used as a beast of burden, was a point lost on the do-gooders. At least they could not object to this particular creature. Instead of the usual donkey ride at Seaburn, a mechanical elephant, seen in the 1950s, was put to use giving children rides along the promenade. The proprietor was known to everyone as Jimmy, though this was not his real name. He was thought to have come from the Gambia, but was brought up by an aunt in Sierra Leona as his mother had died in childbirth. He went to sea as a cabin boy and travelled the world, ending up in Sunderland where he met a local girl from the East End. Their mixed race marriage was unusual for the time. He called himself James Edward George Sawyer and he and his wife moved to a new estate at Southwick in the mid 1920s. He returned to the sea as a member of the Merchant Navy and was twice torpedoed. His petrol driven contraption was an unusual and popular sight just after the war.

Above: 'Are you sitting comfortably? Then we will begin.' That was how those of us now regarded as silver surfers on the internet were introduced to storytime on 'Listen with mother' on the radio. It was expected that we took our places alongside mum on the sofa and concentrated hard on the voice coming over the airwaves at 1.45 every weekday afternoon, just before 'Woman's Hour' came on the Home Service. First broadcast in 1950, the music and voices of Ann Driver, George Dixon and Eileen Browne were welcomed into homes where mother was usually there and not out at work, having dumped her little ones with a child minder. There cannot be many children who did not march up and down the hill with 'The Grand Old Duke of York'. The show ran until 1982, but by then children were placed in front of a TV set and left there for hours on end watching some American tripe or other. 'Story-go-round' was one of the laudable attempts by the Sunderland Library Service to bring back the idea of listening to a story with mum alongside. Librarians, in this case a guitar playing one who could also lead a singsong, went out into the community in an effort to foster a love of literature at a young age.

Top right: If grandpa is lingering too long on this page, get a bucket of cold water ready. Either that or have a large towel on hand to mop his fevered brow. Just look at the

faces on the young lads by the catwalk. Those cheeky grins are there simply because of the bevy of beauty nearby. Those boys are bound to end up like grandpa, still having his head turned by a pretty face, even in his dotage. Still, we must grudgingly admit that the girls were something special and perhaps the female readers have to concede, through gritted teeth, that they had the wow factor. Quite how the judges could possibly rank one above another we will never know as they were all stunners. In the end the vote went to Evelyn Humphrey and, on 4th August 1980, she was presented with the cup, sash, bouquet and the title of 'Miss Sunderland'. It is not known whether Evelyn went on to greater triumphs and Miss World was probably only a dream. Eric Morley began the Miss World Competition in 1951 when Kerstin 'Kiki' Haakonson (pictured below), a Swedish girl, became the first to wear the

crown. The BBC televised Miss World from 1959 to 1979 and Thames Television carried it from 1980 to 1988. At its peak, the show drew in an audience of 27.5 million in Britain alone. We would have a little wager that grandpa was one of the millions watching!

WARTIME

Below: Suits you, sir. Try this one on for size. Looking like some form of 1939 ET, this toddler was being fitted out with a mask as part of the precautions against potential enemy gas attacks during the war. This little one got his piece of defence equipment at Commercial Road School. Chemical warfare was a real fear in the days leading up to what we knew was the inevitable formal declaration of hostilities. A quarter of a century earlier, we had seen at first hand the damage wreaked by mustard gas that was released across the trenches in France and Belgium. This time, we felt that it might be even worse as science had advanced to a degree where even more noxious substances could be turned upon us. Some even mentioned that strains of bubonic plague were ready for release. Fortunately, both sides were so fearful of each other's capability that this form of warfare was never used. Instead, they concentrated on blowing each other to smithereens. The government began its programme of issuing gas masks to the general public during the summer of 1939 and plans were drawn up for a mass evacuation of children from the towns and into the countryside. Babies under two were supplied with a bag-type gas mask, big enough for them to lie in, that was supplied with filtered air by pumping hand bellows. Schoolchildren were issued with gas masks contained in small, six inch cube cardboard boxes, with a piece of string large enough to carry it over the shoulder.

Right: This was the aftermath of just one of the countless raids across Britain during the blitz years in the early 1940s. No one can fully appreciate the sheer feeling of helplessness felt by a person returning from a shelter to discover the ruins of a home unless he has experienced it himself. It was the memories and sentimental possessions that were the biggest losses. Bricks and mortar could be reassembled somewhere else, but the special spot where little Johnny took his first steps or the photographs of a dear departed grandparent were gone forever. This Fulwell householder came back to see what he could salvage after the raid on 13th March 1941. He paints a forlorn picture as he tries to put his whole life's memories and prized possessions into one little suitcase. Even at the time, many people did not appreciate the full story. Those living outside the industrial areas quite often relied on word of mouth to inform them of the human tragedy that was unfolding elsewhere. The press was censored by the government and was not allowed to print some photographs and had to water down part of its reporting in the interests of keeping up morale. Too much honesty might have led to some throwing in the towel and it was important to keep spirits as high as possible with stories of heroism not stark reality.

In the small hours of the morning of 6th September 1940, the German Air Force carried out one of its many raids on the town. On this occasion, the LNER station on Union Street took the brunt of the assault. The roof was blown off, girders crashed to the ground and carriages were gutted, but the most remarkable effect of the explosion was to throw two pairs of carriage wheels high into the air. They crashed down onto B Joseph and Son's sports shop (as can be seen in the picture far right), completing the scene of devastation that the bombs had begun. Fortunately, as it was just after one o'clock in the morning, there were no casualties in this incident. The Empress Hotel nearby remarkably escaped damage, though the staff and residents had taken sensible precautions when the air raid siren sounded and took refuge in the cellar. This was still early days when it came to Sunderland's experience of wartime bombing and some people almost regarded it as an entertainment. Instead of using their brains, like those in the Empress, they would go out into the street to watch the bombs fall and the fires

start. That attitude did not last long as first hand experience of the carnage wreaked by the high explosive on both person and property brought them to their senses. In September 1940, our boys in blue were well into the Battle of Britain as they fought for supremacy in the skies over southern England. The RAF thwarted the Luftwaffe's intention to reduce our aerial defences to a minimum and so pave the way for Hitler's planned invasion of our country. Thanks to the skill, bravery and resolve of our pilots, those plans were put on hold and eventually abandoned. However, the enemy's attention turned to attacking our towns and cities. There had already been a number of attacks from the air, but now The Blitz began in earnest. Not only were industrial centres targeted, but historical sites were focused upon as well in what became known as the 'Baedeker Raids' on cities such as York and Norwich that had little in the way of military value. Sunderland had its shipyards and so knew that it was bound to be in the firing line. Those who had seen the newsreels from the Spanish Civil War and watched film of the air raids during that conflict knew what we could expect. We suffered our first fatalities on 9th August 1940 when three lost their lives at Laing's shipyard.

In April 1941, Binns' department store was ravaged by fire after a direct hit during an air raid in April 1941. As firemen poured gallons of water into the gutted building, plans were already being laid by the owners to keep business going. Obviously, there was no chance of trading from these premises, but within days Binns had secured several outlets across the town from where it could carry on limited trading. This was the sort of spirit that typified the 'we will not be cowed' attitude of both business and the individual during those dark days. The company moved onto Fawcett Street in 1884 and continued expansion saw the store grow to a degree that it could employ 400 people by 1920. By then it had branches across the north of England and in Scotland. Following this air raid, the site was cleared and rebuilding began in late 1949, though it took some four years to complete.

Above: Doxford Shipyard was important to the war effort, as were all Sunderland shipyards that were straining to keep up with the demands of the navy to meet ever tighter deadlines and increase production. The youngster, who is the focus of attention here, looks hardly old enough to be working in such a tough environment. But, there was no easy life for a 14 year old in those days. Lawrence Robinson did not stay in bed, bunk off from school or indulge in hanging round street corners. He was classed as a fully fledged member of the workforce. In 1876, an Act of Parliament decreed that no child under 10 should be at work and school attendance was compulsory. The minimum school leaving age was raised to 11 and then 12 by the end of the century. After World War I, all children had to wait until they were 14 before going out to work and this remained the case until 1947 when a further school year was officially added. Young Lawrence was just a normal member of the shipyard labour force, despite his tender years. Whether or not he fully appreciated the importance of the special visitor who had stopped to chat with him, we do not know. She was the prime minister's wife, Clementine Churchill, and the powerful rock for her husband to lean on during the stressful times of the war.

Bottom: The Women's Voluntary Service was founded as a Civil Defence auxiliary unit in 1938. The WVS gained much experience in providing emergency meals during the second world war, often using the most primitive equipment. WVS mobile canteens served the forces both at home and abroad. During the war years the WVS gained an unforgettable reputation amongst both members of the armed forces and those whose homes had been bombed, always ensuring that cups of tea, sandwiches and cakes were provided exactly where they were needed. When the war ended however members of the WVS had acquired a taste for public service and were unwilling simply to close shop. Distributing

Meals on Wheels on a regular basis to needy people, particularly the elderly, after the war was a new challenge, but one the organisation readily adapted to. In the first six months of 1958, the year when this photograph was taken, the WVS delivered 75,000 such meals - the first course always piping hot from 'Hot Lock' containers. In this picture the WVS are looking delighted at the acquisition of two brand new vans. The fully-fitted vehicles named Cowan and Hanover are gaining the seal of approval from two key figures in WVS. Things had moved a long way from the immediate post-war years when members often delivered meals in their own vehicles.

Left: War had been declared, and every citizen of Britain, young and old, male and female, was called upon to put his or her back into the war effort. Those who did not go into military service of one kind or another worked in factories, dug for victory, gave up their aluminium baths and saucepans, joined organisations and aided in any way they could. These boys from were not going to be left out; they might be too young to fight but while there were sandbags to be filled they were going to do their bit to protect their school building. Thousands of sandbags were used during World War II to protect the country and its beautiful civic buildings.

Above: During World War II, Sunderland was one of the most heavily bombed towns in the country. In total, 267 lost their lives in the air raids that lasted from the summer of 1940 to that of 1943. Some 90 per cent of the housing in the town suffered some form of damage, with as many as 2,000 homes requiring major repairs or complete demolition. This is the aftermath of an attack that took place just after 10 pm on 7th November 1941. The three cottages in the row at 96-98 Fulwell Road were blown to smithereens by the high explosive charge that tore a crater in the ground that measured 15 feet across and was just as deep. Another six houses in the vicinity were damaged. We cannot imagine the terror that must have been felt by those on the receiving end of such attacks. Night after night they heard the sirens and did their best to take cover in Anderson shelters or down in cellars.

Below and right: Barrage balloons were operated by the RAF as an anti-aircraft device designed to protect possible targets from enemy attacks during the war. The barrage balloon was simply a bag of lighter-than-air gas attached to a steel cable anchored to the ground. The balloon could be raised or lowered to the desired altitude by means of a winch. Its purpose was ingenuous: to deny low-level airspace to enemy aircraft. A Balloon Crew originally consisted of two corporals and ten men. As the war progressed, many of the balloons began to be operated by members of the Women's Auxillary Air Force (WAAF), thus releasing men for active service in other areas. The fledgling WAAF was headed by Katherine Jane Trefusis-Forbes with just over 1,700 members stationed throughout the country in 47 Companies. The Air Ministry did not see an immediate need for female assistance throughout the RAF but further defence preparations demonstrated that more staff would be required and some roles such as catering, plotting and operating a teleprinter were considered suitable for women. Telegrams were sent out in August 1939, mobilising all WAAF volunteers and when war was declared on 3rd September, another 10,000 women volunteered. By December 1942 10,000 men had been replaced by some 15,700 WAAF balloon operators. On the home front a group of 'girls' worked extremely hard in very arduous conditions to protect the North East from enemy aerial attacks.The balloons were huge (on average, about 62 feet long and 25 feet in diameter) and it was their job to put up these balloons, which were tethered at various heights on steel cables. The working conditions were difficult and dangerous.

Above: 'What are you doing, mister?' This warden was using the telephone box as a handy resting spot as he filled out some return or checked a particular detail on his log of events. He was a member of the Air Raid Precautions (ARP) team of civilians who offered their services as volunteers on the home front. Many were in jobs that had a protected status as their work expertise was invaluable to wartime production. Others were too old or unfit to join up, but still wanted to play their part. There was also a small handful who just enjoyed being officious and belonged to what came to be known as the 'jobsworth' mentality. Such a type was admirably portrayed by Bill Pertwee as Warden Hodges in the BBC sitcom 'Dad's Army'. During the blackout cries of 'Put that light out' and 'Don't you know there's a war on?' were often mimicked by comedians as part of their variety acts, but most wardens played an important role during the grim days of the early 1940s when we were under attack. They were often in the thick of it, assisting the general public find shelter during an air raid. They also reported the extent of bomb damage and assessed the local need for help from the emergency and rescue services. The wardens used their knowledge of their local areas to help find and reunite family members who had been separated during an air raid.

Below: During World War II all sorts of essential and non-essential foods were rationed, as well as clothing, furniture and petrol. Before the second world war started Britain imported about 55 million tons of food a year from other countries. After war was declared in September 1939, the British government had to cut down on the amount of food it brought in from abroad and decided to introduce a system of rationing. People were encouraged to provide their own food at home. The 'Dig for Victory' campaign started in October 1939 and called for every man and woman to keep an allotment. Lawns and flower-beds were turned into vegetable gardens. Chickens, rabbits, goats and pigs were reared in town parks and gardens. Ration Books were issued to make sure everybody got a fair share. This contained coupons that had to be handed to the shop keepers every time rationed goods were bought. Food was was the first to be rationed. On 8 January 1940, bacon, butter and sugar were rationed. It wasn't just food that was rationed during World War II. Clothing rationing began on June 1st, 1941, two years after food rationing started. There was a shortage of materials to make clothes. People were also urged to 'Make do and mend' so that clothing factories and workers could be used to make items, such as parachutes and uniforms, needed in the battle against Germany. Every item of clothing was given a value in coupons. Each person was given 66 coupons to last them a year. Later it was reduced to 48 coupons. Children were allocated an extra 10 clothing coupons above the standard ration to allow for growing out of clothes during a year. This did not prevent children having to wear 'hand me downs' from older brothers and sisters. In a make do and mend environment, trousers and skirts were patched and darned, Old jumpers were unpicked and the wool used to make new garments. Rationing continued even after the war ended. Fourteen years of food rationing in Britain ended at midnight on 4 July 1954, when restrictions on the sale and purchase of meat and bacon were lifted.

Above: Queen Elizabeth, the wife of King George VI, stood chatting in a relaxed manner to members of the civil defence support services who performed so admirably during the blitz years of the last war. There was major activity for about an hour before and an hour after midnight in the skies on the night of 14th-15th March 1943 over and off the North East coast. There was extensive damage in Sunderland when four PMs and thirty firepot bombs hit the town centre. Bombs were also dropped in many coastal regions. As the clock ticked towards midnight, St Thomas' Church was extensively damaged and, elsewhere in the town, 17 people lost their lives. The Queen was not one to run away or stay at home and hide her face. She went out into the streets to share the people's pain and offer her own encouragement and support. When Buckingham Palace was hit she remarked that now she could face the people in the east end of London as they had a common experience. However, look at the body language of her husband. How stiff and uncomfortable he looked. King George was a shy man, but he could come across as cold. He was lucky to have such a woman at his side as she more than made up for him.

Right: On 8th May 1945 the country learned the news that it had been waiting for. Peace had been declared in Europe and the Nazis were finished. Unbridled scenes of joy and relief were witnessed the length and breadth of the country. Complete strangers grabbed one another and hugged and hugged until they almost burst. In London, crowds gathered by Buckingham Palace and cheered their heads off as the royal family took bow after bow on the balcony. This impromptu dance scene took place in Mowbray Park. Accompanied by a man on a piano accordion, these souls, for whom the word carefree could be used for the first time in years, danced across the flagstones and the grass in a merry whirl of celebration. Their jigs took place in the town's first public park that opened in 1857 on land bought by the Corporation from the Mowbray estate. This was part of a national drive to get people, especially the working classes, out into the open air for a while, away from the insanitary conditions of their homes and the unhealthy atmosphere in the heavy industrial workplaces. Mowbray Gardens was originally known as People's Park and was extended in 1860 to include a lake, terrace and formal gardens. In 2001, a £13 million restoration project was completed that incorporated the Winter Gardens and Museum.

Left: As the second world war came to an end, preparations were made for the celebrations that would see the country go wild with a mixture of relief and excitement when victory in Europe was determined. By April 1945, it was clear that the end was in sight and, when Hitler committed suicide at the end of the month, we knew that it was only a matter of time before we could loose those bluebirds over the white cliffs of Dover. Dorothy Byass was the manageress of Gregg's newsagents, Athenaeum Street. Here she was mounting a display of flags that represent most of the Allied nations who had pitched in to support our battle against fascism. Although the Union flag was the best seller, there was plenty of custom for the maple leaf, stars and stripes and the flags of Australia, New Zealand and all the others who came together in the name of freedom. The Germans offered their unconditional surrender on 7th May in a small schoolhouse near Rheims. The following day, when the news reached these shores, all of Britain took to the streets as all the years of drabness and privation were forgotten. Impromptu congas were danced down Fawcett Street and women kissed complete strangers as they danced across Mowbray Park. In London, the Royal Family was besieged by thousands who flocked to the gates of Buckingham Palace to cheer their Majesties.

AT THE DOCKS

The SS Forthbridge was a 390 feet in length and weighed 5,057 tons. It was managed by Crosby and Sons and completed by W Doxford and Sons in March 1928 for the north of England SS Company and was registered in West Hartlepool. Seen here on the day of its launch, it had provided much needed employment for Wearside shipbuilders during the difficult depression of the interwar years. William Doxford founded his yard in 1840 and his ships were first built at Cox Green. The firm moved to Pallion in 1857 and bought the land there outright in 1870, heralding a stay that would last for over a century. The Doxford name became synonymous with Sunderland shipbuilding, earning that industry's equivalent of the blue riband in 1905 and 1907 when it led the world in production. The 'Grangeberg', an internationally renowned turret ship, was launched from Pallion in 1903. At this time, shipbuilding and repair, marine engineering, coal mining, furniture making and glass manufacture were the major industries that provided Wearside with its wealth. Even immediately after the first world war things were still rosy and Sunderland's 15 yards launched 318,000 tons of shipping in 1920. However, the world recession began to take its toll and in 1926 not a single ship was launched. The 'Forthbridge' was badly damaged by fire in the China Sea in January 1936.

Left: The dockers sat glumly looking out across the river in 1962. The yards that once bustled with energy were lurching to a halt. Austin's was a long established firm, dating back to 1826 when it opened its yard in North Sands. Peter Austin began building wooden colliers and, when his son joined forces with him, moved the business over the river to a spot near Wearmouth Bridge. The depression during the interwar years of the 20th century hit the company badly, but its fortunes revived in the early 1940s because of the need to supply coastal vessels to replace those sunk by enemy U-boats. Austin's also built the frigate 'Amberley Castle' and some landing craft. The difficult times returned when peace was declared and the firm merged with Pickersgill's in 1954. This shipyard closed a decade later and this photograph shows the last ship to have been built there. The company blamed its demise on the decline in the coal trade. The joint venture with Pickersgill continued and a cash injection enabled redevelopment to take place in the 1970s and larger ships could now be constructed. However, an optimistic outlook turned out to be just a pious hope and the Pickersgill part of the operation also closed its yard in the 1980s

Above: Corporation Quay is the principal river berth for the city. It was built by Sunderland Corporation in the 1930s. The quay was designed by Mouchel and Partners, using the Hennebique system of reinforced concrete design, and built by Peter Lind. It is equipped with two 35 ton capacity cranes that have been used to handle forest products, general cargo and steel coils. This view was taken in the 1970s when there was still some traditional employment for dockworkers. The 'Vedra', the main vessel seen here, was built in Paisley and launched on 18th October 1963. Owned by the River Wear Commissioners, it was employed as a bucket dredger, keeping the river clear of silt. The 'Wear Hopper' and the tug 'Pallion' can be seen alongside. The bucket dredge is a very basic, but effective, device that picks up sediment by mechanical means, often with many circulating buckets attached to a wheel or chain. Some of these ships are powerful enough to work through coral reefs to make a shipping channel, though there was hardly any need for that in the North Sea. Ships called 'hoppers' were used to take dirt from the dredgers out into the sea and dispose of it there. The 'Christopher Meeber' is at the quayside, taking on a load of timber. This vessel was built in 1969 for George Peterson of West Germany. The former lifeboat station and slipway is in the distance.

Below: The 'Cleadon' was a tug boat that was built by J Jones of Liverpool in 1899 for the Alexander Towing Company. It was purchased by France Fenwick in 1930 and is seen here passing beneath Wearmouth Bridge in 1954. A year later, it sank off Sunderland Fish Quay, but was raised and continued in service before being scrapped in 1968. Tug boats are strong, highly manoeuvrable craft and have played an important part in the docks, harbours, estuaries and bays around the country. They are remarkable vessels as they deal with shipping many times their own size, teasing and pulling them into position. They are a vital component of any busy port. Before their deployment, muscle and brawn played a major part in getting large boats into position alongside the jetty. Energetic crew members helped line up the vessel in the dock entrance before the ship was towed through using a capstan, usually to the accompaniment of rousing choruses of sea shanties and popular songs. The earliest tugs were fitted with paddle wheels but these were soon replaced by a propeller driven system that relied on steam and, latterly, diesel. Today's large ships cannot easily manoeuvre within the close confines of some ports as their turning circles are too large and they cannot maintain enough speed for their rudders to be fully effective. They need the help of tugs.

Right: As the 1930s got under way, the seemingly active port of Sunderland was going through a bad patch, despite the evidence of this aerial photograph that suggests a hive of activity. The interwar years were difficult ones for those who relied on what had become traditional industries, born of the industrial revolution and growth during the Victorian age. A quarter of the working classes found itself idle and many families had to exist below the poverty line. Coal, iron, steel and shipbuilding, all those that were at the heart of life in much of Wales, Scotland, Northern Ireland and the North of England, went into a massive decline. These industries had struggled after the 1914-18 war as they had failed, for one reason or another, to modernise and stiff competition from overseas saw them start to crumble. As men stood around looking lost and despairing as to how they could feed their loved ones, a different picture emerged further south. New light industries, such as chemicals, electrical goods and automobiles had been developed. Workers and managers in these areas prospered and enjoyed a level of affluence that split Britain in two as a nation separated by the great divide of the haves and the have nots. The government of the day lacked vision and inspiration, seeming powerless in formulating policies that could effectively counter the hardship suffered by so many.

SPORT

We now have our Stadium of Light on the north bank of the Wear, but older soccer fans will tell you that the Stadium Shout does not compare with the Roker Roar of yesteryear. Truth to tell, there has not been a great deal to shout or roar about in recent times as our soccer club has bounced up and down between the two top divisions like the rubber ball that Bobby Vee sang about nearly half a century ago. This is how Roker Park looked in 1936, coincidentally the year in which we last won the old Division One championship. When the ground was officially opened on 10th September 1898, the Marquis of Londonderry paid homage to the Henderson brothers who had brokered a deal to build it on farmland, provided that housing would be built there too. The construction process took less than a year and 30,000 people turned up to watch the first match when Liverpool were the visitors. The Hendersons were directors of the club that previously played at Newcastle Road, but knew that it was wasting opportunities to develop Sunderland into a major force unless a larger and more modern home could be found. The club was originally one for schoolteachers, but this rule was relaxed in 1881 and it turned professional in 1885. Roker Park eventually reached 75,000 capacity, but safety measures reduced this considerably in later years and in 1997 the fans moved down the road to Monkwearmouth.

Below: These bills were used to advertise a pair of boxing cards in the 1930s. The left hand one had Douglas Parker topping the bill at Sunderland's Holmeside Stadium on 12th April 1930. Important fights were over 15 rounds, as opposed to the maximum of 12 today. Parker went on to hold the Northern Area lightweight title 1933-35. Born in Aberdeen, he joined a boxing booth as part of a travelling fair. It was a tough upbringing as he would have several fights each evening against challengers who might weigh quite a bit more than he did. However, his skills usually meant that the fight was short as his opponents over estimated their own abilities. When the show arrived in Sunderland he decided to make the town his base and joined the official professional ranks in the late 1920s. In 1930 he was a busy man, fitting in 15 bouts over that 12 month period. This match against Frank Markey saw Parker win on points, avenging an earlier defeat. He retired at the end of 1935 having hit a losing streak. He died in 1965. The other bill comes from 2nd September 1938 when Tom Smith beat Norman Denny on points. Born on 26th September 1918, Smith turned professional a month before his 16th birthday, earning 7s 6d (37.5p) for a four round contest. He became the Northern Area featherweight champion 1940-43 and British Army lightweight champion 1944-45. Smith died in 1990.

Right: Sunderland was one of the country's top soccer sides in the late 1930s. It finished runner up in Division One in 1935 and lifted the title the following year. In 1937, the Roker men went all the way to Wembley in the FA Cup and overcame 'proud' Preston North End after conceding the first goal. Strikes from Gurney, Carter and Burbanks sealed a 3-1 victory. The homecoming on Fawcett Street was memorable. The space outside the Town Hall was packed with supporters who cheered their heroes to the heavens. Every vantage place was occupied, including the balcony outside Meng's Restaurant. This was a prestigious establishment that sadly closed in 1952. Until then, from its opening in 1889, it had enjoyed a fine reputation as the place to dine in the town. Many a bride and groom held their wedding reception inside its doors. The ladies who lunch brigade of yesteryear found it a popular spot in which to relax from the rigours of shopping. They would not have been too concerned about the merits of the WM formation of the soccer team, but there were thousands on Fawcett Street that day who did.

Top right: Notice that there is not an earring in sight. Additionally, if any of these men had a tattoo, then it would have been of an anchor and not some weird Celtic symbol. They also had never heard of a metatarsal, especially as they wore proper boots and not the carpet slippers that the modern fancy Dan puts on and then wonders why his foot hurts when someone treads in it. These lads did not drive smart sports cars. They travelled to soccer matches on the same buses that brought the fans in. The only

clubbing that they got involved in was at the British Legion or the working man's club. There were no special tactics for this eleven. Fullbacks kicked wingers over the touchline and centre forwards took the ball, goalkeeper and anything else in their way into the back of the net. Wing halves and inside forwards were allowed to do a little bit of trickery until the crowd got fed up and urged them to 'get rid'. This Sunderland team was ready to do battle in the 1938-39 season, the last before the second world war broke out and thus finished the careers of several of these players. Among the more illustrious names who have worn the red and white stripes was Horatio (Raich) Carter, then the youngest man to have captained the Division One champions when, aged 23, he led Sunderland to glory in 1936.

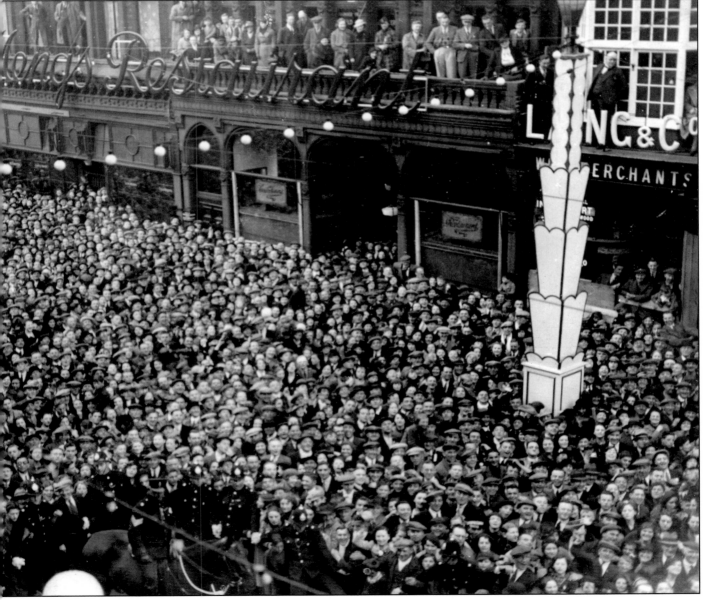

Below: It was standing room only for most of the supporters at Roker Park. In the days of terraces and flat caps and not a designer replica kit in sight, games kicked off at 3 pm on a Saturday. Midweek games were occasional affairs and the Sabbath was for going to church. The crowd was almost exclusively male, but it was a protective one. Young lads were shepherded down to the front where they could get a better view. They rejoined dad at half time for a cup of Bovril before returning to press their noses up against the railings. When the players ran on to the field there were just 11 of them to a side. The manager took his place in the dugout alongside the trainer who carried his bucket and magic sponge. No substitutes were allowed, so this pair could concentrate on seeing that those on the field carried out the pre-match instructions. Tactics were straightforward. Kick him before he kicks you and do not play silly beggars in front of goal.

Right: Who would have believed it possible, but a dream really had come true. Anyone at Wembley on that Saturday in May, or watching on the television at home, will remember the leaping Bob Stokoe as he bounded like a giraffe on ecstasy across the hallowed turf to greet Jim Montgomery. Manager and goalkeeper threw their arms around each other as they shared both elation and disbelief that the mighty Leeds United had just been turned over. Ian Porterfield scored the vital goal when he drilled home a shot past the despairing dive of David Harvey after half an hour. Porterfield, who died in September 2007, is something of a Trivial Pursuit quiz question in himself as he is the last person to succeed Alex Ferguson as a manager. He took over at Aberdeen in 1986. Leeds threw what they could at the Sunderland goal, but the defence held firm, none more so than Montgomery. His amazing double save from Trevor Cherry and Peter Lorimer was straight from Boy's Own.

departed as manager and was replaced temporarily by Billy Elliot. The board appointed Bob Stokoe as manager at the start of the 1972-73 season in what proved to be an inspired move. As a former Newcastle United centre half, there were a few eyebrows raised about the wisdom of such a move, but Stokoe was soon to win the hearts of the Wearsiders. The league season proved to be moderately successful as our boys ended in sixth position, but it was the glamour of the FA Cup that made the year so memorable. The legendary run through to the final began in the cold days of winter and came to an end on 5th

When the final whistle went, the twin towers were rocked to their foundations by the volume of the Wearside roar. It was repeated when 'the little general', Scotland's Bobby Kerr, lifted the FA Cup. Kerr served Sunderland faithfully for 15 years, before ending his career with short stints at Blackpool and Hartlepool. Since then he has worked in several places across the region as a publican, including one hostelry in Houghton-le-Spring.

Below: That was the year that was. In 1972, Sunderland was languishing in Division Two of the Football League. Alan Brown

May at Wembley. Some good sides had been beaten along the route, but lying in wait was the monster known as Leeds United. Third in Division One, the Yorkshire outfit was the hottest favourite for donkeys' years. Although the Roker Park boys were the darlings of the neutrals as Leeds' manager, Don Revie, and his side were loathed by most for their gamesmanship and tendency to bully referees, few gave us a real chance. In their heart of hearts even our own faithful knew that we were just turning up to complete the numbers. These faces show that miracles do happen as we won 1-0.

Brian Havelock & Russ Dent

Speedway images courtesy of www.newcastlespeedwayhistory.co.uk

Top: Action from the Boldon track in 1974 with Brian Havelock and Russ Dent out in front and look to be heading towards a 5-1 home win. This was to be Sunderland's last season in Speedway and Brian 'Havvy' Havelock has the dubious honour of winning the last ever race at the track. Russ Dent 'The Skipper' rode in all four seasons that Sunderland 'Stars'/ 'Gladiators' competed in the British League second division, between 1971 and 1974. During his time at the club he rightly deserved the title of 'Mr Sunderland Speedway' as he rode in more matches, had more rides and scored more points than anyone else.

Above: The tapes originally went up on the first ever speedway meeting held at Boldon Stadium on 21st April 1964. A challenge match between the 'Saints' and famous local rivals the Newcastle Diamonds, who at the time included Ivan Mauger and Russ Dent. Mauger went onto be multiple world champion and Dent skippered the Sunderland side in the 70s.

Although 'Saints' won the opening heat they lost the match by a 32-44 scoreline. Sadly only a couple of months later Sunderland speedway was closed and it would be another seven years before the sound of speedway machines were to be heard again at the Boldon track.

Below: Action from Sunderland Russ Dent (gate 4) and George Barclay (gate 2), 1972.

Below: One of the rewards for winning promotion to the top division in 1980 was a trip to Norway. There the players could mix pleasure and soccer as they played the odd game that was merely a friendly conducted at a gentle pace. They travelled over there by coach and looked to be eagerly anticipating the occasion. Even though the boys were paid a decent wage for their efforts, they were still a long way from players of the 21st century. Although they would soon be rubbing shoulders with the top teams such as Liverpool, Manchester United and Arsenal, even the players from those sides could not rely on a footballer's pay packet being a meal ticket for life. Some of the men in the photograph found employment as coaches or match day hosts after they retired, but for most it was off into civvy street to look for a job with, for many, little in the way of formal training or qualifications. One who did make it into the higher echelons of the soccer hierarchy is pictured four from the right at the back. Whisper his name around here. It is Sam Allardyce, the man who became manager of Newcastle in 2007.

Players: Arnott, Rowell, Chisholm, Cooke, Cummins, Marangoni, Dunn, Brown, Turner, Hindmarsh, Buckley, Allardyce, Hawley, Hinnigan, Whitworth

Bottom: This photograph was taken from the match against Everton at the start of the 1980-81 season. Under the managership of Ken Knighton, Sunderland had won promotion from Division Two and entered the new decade full of hope, but it was to be yet another period that was not for the faint hearted. Relegated in 1985, the fans were shocked to the core when, two years later, a play off match was lost that consigned us to Division Three until the Marco Gabbiadini goalscoring rescue act helped us back up in 1988.

EVENTS
&
OCCASIONS

'Goodbye cruel world, I'm off to join the circus'. Pop pickers from the 1960s might recall the words of the song that was a minor hit in this country for an American heartthrob, actor and singer James Darren. This photograph taken on High Street West, though, dates from long before he was ever thought of as it was taken c1900. This circus, as well as countless others that followed it, would have been more likely to associate itself with the music of the Czech composer, Julius Fucik. His rousing march, 'Entry of the Gladiators' was picked up by many such entertainers and used as the introductory overture to their shows. When the circus came to town, the immediate period before opening night was always a grand spectacle. Gaily covered floats advertising the dates and times of the performances made their way in a procession along the streets. Following along behind were outlandishly dressed clowns, lurching along in their big shoes, merrily squirting water over the watching crowd lining the streets. Acrobats tumbled their way along the road, performing flip flops and cartwheels as they went. Pretty girls in sequinned costumes waved to the onlookers and jugglers tossed Indian clubs high into the air and men on stilts doffed their tall hats as they went by. An elephant, with a turbaned rider aloft, brought up the rear.

Right: It had been a long time coming, but the last of our boys had made it home. This civic reception was held in their honour as the town said a heartfelt thanks for their service and their relatives breathed a sigh of relief that normality could return. These men were survivors from the Sunderland 125 Anti Tank Regiment who were captured in Singapore when the island fell to the Japanese in February 1942. First colonised by the East India Company in 1819, it was an important trading outpost along the spice route. In the 20th century it had considerable military significance because of its Asian position. The British based there were ill prepared for the concerted attack by the Japanese and Singapore fell in just six days. The supposed 'Bastion of the Empire' was in enemy hands and the shockwaves went all the way back to London.

Below: Chestnuts roasting, Rudolph pawing the ground and the little elves beavering away in Santa's workshop; as Noddy Holder shouted at the end of Slade's biggest ever hit song, 'It's Christmas'. Blandford Street was getting ready for the festivities as lights were put up on Christmas trees and hung in strings above the pavements and across the street. Stars twinkled brightly and no one minded the cold as they got ready for the season of good cheer. Seen in the 1970s, shopping continued here much as it had in previous decades. The shopping mall was still not really established in many places, but

it was on the way. The Bridges Centre would eventually dominate the area close to here. Many of our gifts are chosen there now, but 30 or more years ago we were still able to drift from shop top shop and street to street in search of that special

present or stocking filler. Little ones just loved a trip to see Father Christmas, even if he did seem to have lost three stone in weight since he came to their school the previous Friday. Mums enjoyed seeing the look of wonder and joy on their children's faces as the old man with the white beard patted them on the head benignly. Some Santas who had a twinkle in their eye invited mum to sit on their knee, but it was all friendly banter and no one took offence.

Once upon a time we had a Town Hall of which we could be proud. It stood halfway along Fawcett Street and imposed its grandeur and splendour on all who witnessed it. Even when we were elsewhere in town the chimes of its lovely clock could be heard form several hundred yards away, reminding us of its presence. What do we have now as a symbol of local government? Something called a Civic Centre, created from concrete and glass that could double as a car park, will never match the edifice that was swept away in 1971 in the name of progress. Sir Basil Spence, of Coventry Cathedral fame, may have designed its replacement, but he could never match the sheer sense of awe one had when gazing upon the Fawcett Street building that opened on 6th November 1890. Designed by local brothers John and Thomas Tillman, the Town Hall was rather late in arriving on the scene as a centre for council business, in comparison with other towns. Since 1835, meetings were held in the Exchange Building, but it was not until 1873 that it was decided to hold a competition to select an architect and design that would provide an appropriate setting for the council. Even then, it took 10 years to acquire the eventual site and a new competition had to be launched since previous competitors had moved on. Seen here in 1937, the building was decorated for the coronation celebrations that took place when George VI officially became our monarch.

The area around the Fawcett Street corner with Borough Road and Mowbray Park has been remodelled with the recreation of the Museum and Winter Gardens in 2001, thanks in part to lottery funding. The museum was opened in 1852, the first municipally funded one outside London. Its move four years later to its home by Mowbray Park saw the inclusion of the Winter Gardens that were modelled on the Crystal Palace. The American President, Ulysses Grant was present at the opening ceremony. The Winter Garden building was badly damaged in

1941 during one of the many air raids and had to be demolished the following year. A replacement extension to the museum was not built until the 1960s. Seen in this attractive night time view across the park's lake, the buildings were illuminated as part of the celebrations for the coronation of George VI on 12th May 1937. This was the date originally earmarked for his brother, Edward VIII, but he had abdicated the previous December, propelling the new king into a limelight for which he was unprepared and reluctant to assume. But, duty called and he took up the reins of the monarchy.

Above: Trestle tables were borrowed from church halls and schoolrooms. Out came the tablecloth from the bottom drawer in the sideboard as dining room and kitchen chairs were dragged out into the street. It was party time. Mums baked buns and cakes. Margarine was spread on the sandwiches and every last ration coupon went to make this a day to remember. It was VE Day. On 8th May 1945 all Britain took to the streets. After nearly six long years the war in Europe was over and, just for a while, the drab years were forgotten. A blaze of multi coloured flags, fireworks and decorations celebrated the great day. Scenes like this were repeated in every street in the land. Party hats were hurriedly made and the children given a treat the like they had not known since the 1930s. Some women shed a quiet tear for the sweetheart or father who would not be coming home. For each one who looked forward to the day she would be reunited with her husband there was another who knew that hers lay in a foreign field. In the town centre people went mad. They hugged total strangers and kissed policemen. Similar scenes were repeated two months later when the war with Japan ended. In the meantime, pass the lemonade and let's have three cheers for our brave lads overseas.

Above right: The Queen and Duke of Edinburgh visited on 29th October 1954. She had only been our monarch for less than two years and her coronation in June the previous year was still fresh in everyone's memory. Her handsome, if at times irascible husband, as ever stood one step behind Her Majesty as she gave all in the Town Hall the benefit of her radiant smile. The monarchy was at its height of popularity in those days as the country began to emerge from postwar austerity and look forward with eager anticipation to a new Elizabethan age. The Lord Lieutenant of Durham is the uniformed man next to her. He was a significant figure in the north east. John James Lawson (1881-1965), known to everybody as Jack, was born into poverty to illiterate parents in Whitehaven. Despite this humble background, Jack was schooled from an early age and developed a love of reading. The family moved to Durham where his father got work in the mines and became a committed trade unionist. Jack followed his father down the pit and became a committed socialist. He continued his education via correspondence courses and eventually won a place at Oxford. He developed political ambitions and became the MP for Chester le Street in 1919. His star continued to rise and in 1939 became Deputy Commissioner for Civil Defence in the Northern Region. He was Secretary of State for War in Clement Attlee's postwar Cabinet and was elevated to the title Lord Lawson of Beamish in 1950.

Below: It seems remarkable that in a few years' time it will be half a century since this group of young Scousers took the pop world by storm. George, John, Ringo and Paul were only finalised as the line up of the Beatles a few months before the release of their first single, 'Love me do' in late 1962. Pete Best had just been discarded as the drummer and Stuart Sutcliffe had died earlier in the year, turning the quintet into the Fab Four as we came to know them. Music on Merseyside spawned several big names in the early 1960s and the Beatles were not among them. Gerry and the Pacemakers was the top group and ballad singer Billy Fury an already well established artist with a string of hits. The Beatles, lurched into the top 20 with their debut disc. However, after that, their success was all down to their popularity. Even so, when they came to perform at the Sunderland Empire on Saturday, 9th February 1963, it was teen sensation Helen Shapiro who topped the bill. 'Please please me' gave the mopheads their first really big hit and they followed it up with their first number one, 'From me to you'. After that, it was 'yeah, yeah, yeah' all the way.

TRANSPORT

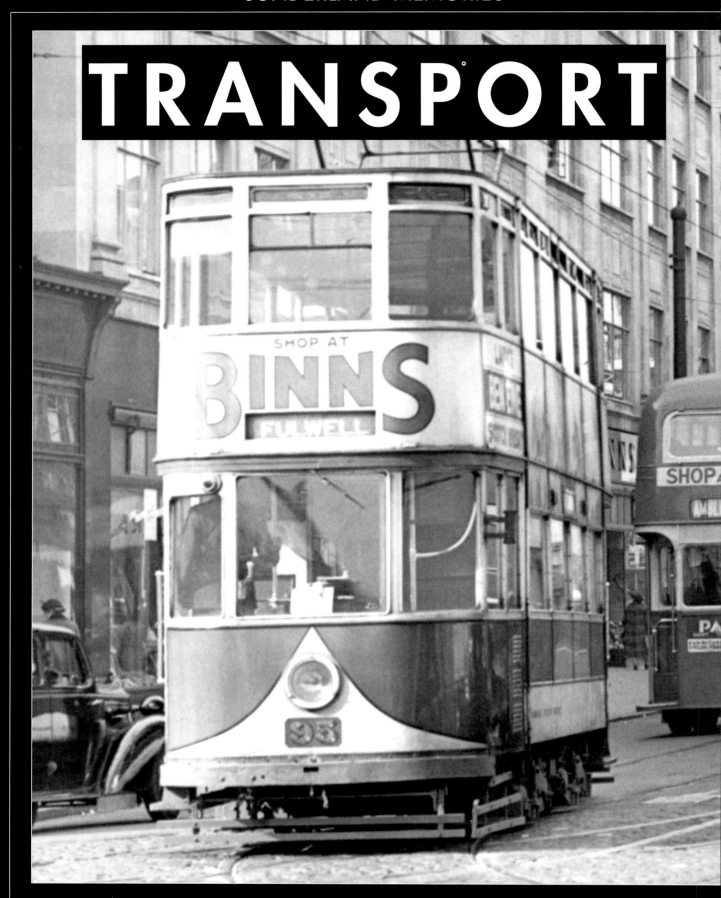

Seen at Gas Office Corner, the No 95 tram was just about to turn the corner out of Fawcett Street as it passed Binns' department store. Built by English Electric in 1933, it survived for the remainder of its service life that was brought to an end when the last ones made their final journeys in procession on 1st October 1954. This photograph was taken just six months before that day when passengers took their last rides at a cost of one shilling (5p). By this time, the tram service was limited to the Borough Road to Seaburn route. When the historic vehicles were finally declared redundant, most had an inauspicious end in the scrapyard. One that did escape has had a new lease of life. No 16, built in Preston in 1900, somehow made its way to a football field where it was used as a changing room. Later, the lower saloon ended up at Westwood Farm, near Hexham, where it was incongruously used as a tool shed and apple store. After 30 years there, it was discovered by the Beamish Tramway Group who lovingly restored it and set it to work in the open air museum that is near Stanley. Sunderland's Kate Adie, the BBC reporter, presided at the tram's official return to duty in July 2003.

Above It was not so much a penny for your thoughts as a penny farthing for them. Dressed in period costume, this rider bowled along Durham Road, opposite the houses on Tanfield Road, Thorney Close. The workmen must have thought that they had seen some form of Adam Adamant reappearing from a bygone age before their very eyes, as Arthur Askey might have put it. The high wheel bicycle, or penny farthing as it was nicknamed for obvious reasons, helped promote the popularity of cycling as a sport and a recreation. First seen in 1870, it was the first true bicycle that was designed for both speed and distance. In the absence of a gearing system, ever larger front wheels were tried in order to achieve this aim. It replaced the velocipede, known as the 'boneshaker' because of the quality of ride it gave, that was invented by Pierre Lallement in 1863. The penny farthing was difficult to stop and on long downhill stretches it was recommended that riders take their feet off the pedals and hook them over the handlebars, so that in case of a crash they would land (hopefully) on their feet! This made for quick descents but left almost no chance of stopping should the need arise. After Dunlop's invention of the pneumatic tyre in 1887, smaller chain driven bicycles replaced the high wheel variety.

Below: These lorries were among the first to be used by the Sunderland Gas Company, Commercial Road. They carried the slogan 'use gas coke and avoid smoke' in an attempt to attract business, but at the same time make the point about the soot laden skies that covered our industrial centres in those days. Residents coughed and spluttered in such an environment and it was impossible to keep shirt collars and cuffs clean for a day. Even washing hung on the line would often be ruined by black flecks if left out too long. It was not until a succession of Clean Air Acts in the 1950s that our polluted urban areas became healthier places to be. Older readers will recall wearing face masks as they struggled through the smog to get to work or to school. These lorries were based at Hendon Gas Works as their drivers posed for this promotional photograph. It was back in 1667 that Thomas Shirley noticed inflammable gas leaking from a coal deposit on a Wigan coalfield and John Clayton produced the first coal gas in 1684 and stored it in animal bladders. However, after over a century of experiment, it was not until 1806 that a Manchester cotton mill was lit by gas and London's Pall Mall the following year. Gas was first used to illuminate some of Sunderland's streets in 1824.

Above and below: An unusual sight at any time but here we see a Norwegian flying boat landing on the Wear in 1947. On the evening of June 30th 1947 thousands of Wearsiders crowded the harbour front to watch as the first Catalina flying boat to land at Sunderland. Operated by the Norwegian airline, Vingtor Luftveier, the flying boat had flown from Gothenburg with a mission to bring the crew of 24 of the Swedish steamer 'Aida', to Sunderland. The 'Aida' had been built at Pallion by Short Brothers' shipyard and was ready for her maiden voyage. Crewing the flying boat were ex-RAF Squadron Leader Thomas Maxwell-Hudson, Flight Engineer Charles Jones and Captain Hudson, together with four Norwegian airmen – all of whom had enjoyed distinguished service with the RAF during World War Two. Spectators cheered and waved from the old North Pier as the aircraft taxied between the inner piers towards the lower buoys and the task of bringing the crimson and cream Catalina into the Wear and ensuring a safe mooring fell to river pilot Leslie Dodds. Passengers and aircrew were then ferried across the river to Corporation Quay. Mr SC Wright, Swedish Consul for Sunderland, greeted the seafarers, who were afterwards taken to the local Mission to Seamen prior to joining Aida. Owned by Stockholm-based Rederi Ab Soya, the 435-foot long cargo ship had a relatively short-lived career. After being sold to Panamanian owners in 1949 and renamed Naida, she sank following a collision at Alexandria, Egypt, in 1958. The Catalina was one of two identical flying boats in Vingtor's fleet which operated air taxi services. Sadly, the flying boat pictured suffered an untimely fate as she was written-off during a crash landing on August 5th 1947.

Above: The northeast has a particular pride of place in the history of the locomotive. The Stockton to Darlington railway that opened in 1825 was the world's first permanent steam locomotive railway. On that inaugural day, some 600 passengers were carried, most of them in coal trucks, on that 26 mile journey. Over a century later, this A1 class 'Boswell' locomotive passed through Monkwearmouth Station with a parcels train bound for York. It was now 1960 and the great days of steam were largely over. Diesel and electricity were to be the power sources that British Rail would rely on in the future. Those days of the 1930s, when the likes of 'Cheltenham Flyer', 'Flying Scotsman', 'Silver Jubilee' and 'Coronation Scot' thundered down the line were well in the past. Their record breaking attempts kept the nation enthralled as the 100 mph barrier was eventually smashed. The successive feats culminated in the remarkable 126 mph reached by 'Mallard' in 1938. The magic of steam even inspired Eric Coates to compose 'Coronation Scot' as a tribute to the prowess of that locomotive. Followers of 'Paul Temple', the detective series that was a popular radio broadcast, will recall that this piece was used as the signature tune. Literature also responded to the stimulus, as with the poet WH Auden who used the cadence of a train running at speed to provide the metre for his atmospheric 'Night Mail'.

Left: St Mary's RC Church on Bridge Street provided the backdrop for this view across the Wearmouth Bridge in 1979. From the age of the cars crossing the river, it would seem that they were part of some motorcade of an owners' club as the registration plates suggest that the vehicles dated back to the 1950s and earlier. Crossing the bridge on a sunny day has some drivers feeling as if they were being flashed by strobe lighting as alternative shafts of light and shadow appear on the roadway through the girders and struts of the structure. This is the latest of the bridges that have crossed the Wear on or about this point. It dates from 1928-29 and replaced the one designed by Robert Stephenson that had stood here for 70 years. The very first one in place was a remarkable piece of engineering. Completed in 1796, it was only the second iron bridge that anyone had seen, the first being in Coalbrookdale, Shropshire. As there had been no through road to Newcastle, ferries used to carry people and goods over the waters. When the river was in spate or the boats were overloaded, this was a dangerous venture. For many years people had wondered about bridging the Wear, but a normal structure would not have enough height to let the colliers sail below. However, the successful bridging of the Severn provided Wearside with its chance to do the same.

Above: Seen at Grangetown, these two were arch rivals for space on the roads. The contest would be won by the bus when trams were retired in 1954. The single decker was a Northern Guy Arab on the No 23 route to Dawdon. The No 38 tram, formerly part of the Huddersfield fleet, was heading for Fulwell. The first trams that ran in Sunderland were built in Preston at the Dick Kerr factory. In all, 18 cars were built in 1900 for the Corporation. Twelve of these were 56 seat, four-wheel, open top double deck vehicles made to the maker's standard design with three saloon windows each side. The other six were longer models, with six saloon windows per side, seating 64 passengers and mounted on bogies to the American Brill Company's 22E design. The slightly superior vehicles were intended for the Christ Church to Roker route as this journey was considered to be the prestigious one. Work on laying track and erecting cabling moved quickly, so that by February 1901 the Circle route was fully operational. This served the districts to the west of the town that were made up of industrial sites and high density housing. Very soon, this attracted considerably more patronage than the north-south main line.

SHOPPING
SPREE

By 1923 the war had been over for nearly five years, but its effects lingered on. The world economy struggled to cope with a recession that was beginning to bite hard. In Germany, the standing of the mark was so pitiful that people could carry their almost worthless banknotes around in a wheelbarrow, such was the level of devaluation. Before the end of the decade the Wall Street stock market in America would crash, turning millionaires into bankrupts overnight. At home, things were little better. Lloyd George had promised the population that the government would create a 'land fit for heroes'. There was little evidence of that. Wages were low and jobs would soon become more difficult to find. Little wonder that families did their best to get along as well as they could, but for many at the bottom end of the social scale it was a case of living hand to mouth. Sunderland Old Market was a popular spot to try to make the family purse stretch that much further. It was the main walk through market in the east end of town. It welcomed its first shoppers in August 1830 and by the time of its centenary boasted 47 shops and 19 stalls. A celebratory procession was held to mark that occasion, led by the mayor, and a fancy dress parade was judged by the Stockton comedian, Jimmy James.

Below: If you thought that traffic congestion was a modern phenomenon, think again. Over half a century ago our towns and cities started to feel the strain as car ownership increased and scenes like this one in March 1953 became commonplace. Although some of the landmarks pictured here are no longer with us, such as the Bells public house, the Grand Hotel and Share furniture shop, this is quite clearly Mackie's Corner. The tramlines swept around the corner into High Street West and onwards towards the terminus outside the railway station. The mix of buses, trams, cars and lorries made it a nightmare, but the volume of traffic was nothing compared to the amount of traffic that we have to cope with today. One way systems, pedestrianisation, tolls and parking restrictions have been tried in different places and, although they have helped make town centres more user friendly, all they have done is move the problem to the perimeters. At the time of this photograph people were thinking ahead to the Queen's coronation in June and what a grand celebration that would be. However, there was some sadness connected with the planning as her grandmother, Queen Mary, passed away this month.

Above: In 1956, Union Street Market closed for business. This was the last day of trading and shoppers were anxious to get an even better bargain than usual, knowing that there would be some heavy price reductions as traders attempted to get rid of as much stock as they could. This site is part of where the The Bridges Shopping Centre now stands. Open air markets, though, have a special atmosphere that cannot be matched by any indoor establishment. There are characters manning the stalls with witticisms and homespun philosophy to charm and amuse their customers. It is hard work getting up early in the morning and getting down to the wholesalers and coming back to the stall to set up for the day, but the stallholders got used to it. This was their way of life and the friendly banter with housewives looking to fill their shopping baskets was all part of normal business practice. Contrast the attitude of a greengrocer offering a pound of bananas for sale with that of a pimply youth on a supermarket checkout. Apart from the fact that he would be slung into prison for mentioning imperial measures such as pounds and ounces, our cheeky chappie would get you to part with your money by suggesting that they would perk the old man up. The lad on the till just grunts, 'Need any help with your packing?' What, help to put a pound (sorry - half kilo) of bananas in a bag?

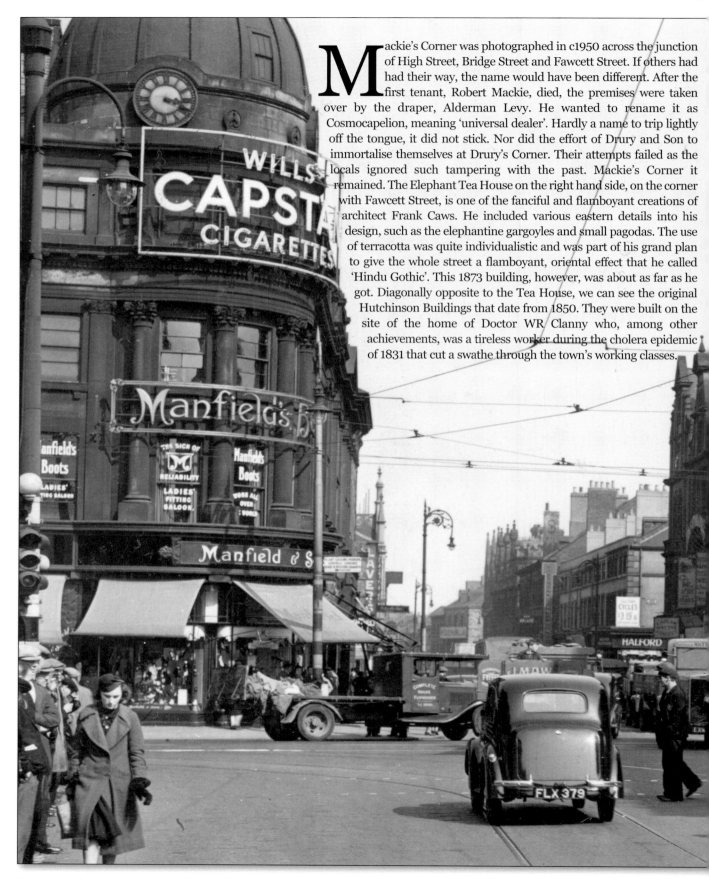

Mackie's Corner was photographed in c1950 across the junction of High Street, Bridge Street and Fawcett Street. If others had had their way, the name would have been different. After the first tenant, Robert Mackie, died, the premises were taken over by the draper, Alderman Levy. He wanted to rename it as Cosmocapelion, meaning 'universal dealer'. Hardly a name to trip lightly off the tongue, it did not stick. Nor did the effort of Drury and Son to immortalise themselves at Drury's Corner. Their attempts failed as the locals ignored such tampering with the past. Mackie's Corner it remained. The Elephant Tea House on the right hand side, on the corner with Fawcett Street, is one of the fanciful and flamboyant creations of architect Frank Caws. He included various eastern details into his design, such as the elephantine gargoyles and small pagodas. The use of terracotta was quite individualistic and was part of his grand plan to give the whole street a flamboyant, oriental effect that he called 'Hindu Gothic'. This 1873 building, however, was about as far as he got. Diagonally opposite to the Tea House, we can see the original Hutchinson Buildings that date from 1850. They were built on the site of the home of Doctor WR Clanny who, among other achievements, was a tireless worker during the cholera epidemic of 1831 that cut a swathe through the town's working classes.

Right: In November 1960 it was good to get in out of the cold. St Thomas' Street Arcade provided some shelter from the elements, though it could still be draughty along here. The woman in the foreground peered into Palmer's shop window as she thought about a Christmas present for one of her children. There were plenty of Dinky cars and Rosebud dolls to catch the eye. The company grew from humble beginnings as a music shop into a large multiple store. This mother's pram looks as if it had done good service. This woman and her counterpart, who was gazing into the Scottish Knitting Company window, never dreamed of coming into town bareheaded. Hence, they produced the ubiquitous headscarf. A proper lady always wore something on her head, unlike some flighty pieces they could mention. This shopping area was called the New Arcade' when it opened in 1874. Marks and Spencer had a penny bazaar here at the turn into the 20th century. The arcade was badly damaged in an air raid in 1943 and was not fully reopened until July 1951. It was later demolished and replaced by a telephone exchange.

Left: Looking at the woolly clothing, warm hats and sheepskin linings, it is hard to imagine that this is the first half of the swinging 60s when boutiques became the rage and hemlines became little more than pelmets. Taken from Green Street, the photograph shows shops on High Street West as we look eastwards. Although you would not imagine it from this scene, there really was a revolution in fashion, popular music and social attitudes taking place on our streets and in our homes. We entered this decade full of optimism as the largely austere 1950s were now behind us and we embarked on the 'never had it so good' era that Harold Macmillan assured us we were experiencing. There was truth in the remark as unemployment was low and wage packets bulged. Young people felt the change as well, coming to realise that their new found wealth gave them a power not fully experienced by parents who grew up in the depressed times of the interwar years. Mary Quant opened a shop in London that was aimed at a youthful market. Young women were not content to dress like their mothers did and found their own self expression in mini skirts and kinky boots.

Above: An every day shopping scene dating from 1968 is featured in this delightful picture. The smart shop on this busy corner belonged to A.Healey Graham Ltd., it was located next to the equally popular Stewart Brothers fireplace shop and further along the street Leveys wallpaper stores. The 1960s fashions are apparent in the photograph, note the young lady crossing the road on the left, wearing the 'slacks' with the straps under the arches of her feet that were so popular at the time. The Vauxhall Viva at the front of the row of parked cars was epitome of the new style of affordable saloon cars with sleek, clean lines and rectangular headlamps which characterised the late 1960s and 1970s. Sunderland's inner ring road was constructed in 1968; this caused much disruption and upset through the town. The first section of the new road linked Bridge Street with a modern roundabout on the junction of High Street West and Gill Bridge Avenue. Much of the property along Bridge Street was pulled down, including the Bridge End Vaults, Kennedy's store and the Rose and Crown public house.

WORKING LIFE

Women played a major role during the last war as they filled the gaps left by men who had been called up on active service. Production had to be maintained in their absence and Land Army girls flocked to the countryside to bring in the harvest and tend to the livestock. Others kept public transport services going by driving buses and trams, while some got behind the wheels of ambulances.

Many joined up officially and donned uniforms, acting as support personnel in radar tracking stations or even flying Spitfires from Southampton to airbases where they were needed by the RAF to mount a defence of our realm. Others went into civil defence positions, arranging salvage collections or offering support to those affected in the air raids. These women in the photograph took over jobs as welders, builders and repair hands in the shipyards. It was tough work, but someone had to do it to keep the wheels of industry turning. Their mothers had performed similar tasks in the previous war, so there was already a precedent set. However, for some the crunch came in peacetime. There were quite a few who could not accept that it was their niche in life to return to the kitchen sink and don an apron once more. They had tasted the outside world and wanted more of it.

Right: Dublin has Molly Malone with her wheelbarrow, cockles and mussels. Sunderland had Maggie O'Hare, though her real name was Mrs Bulmer. She was one of the last of the fishwives who once graced the East End. They filleted the fish in the streets and were particularly popular with local cats that congregated around their pitches, hunting for scraps. The women went off through the street selling their wares and often called into local pubs to try to make a few shillings by persuading the drinkers that they needed some fresh fish or shellfish to take home to their own wives. Margaret (Meg) Shipley was another well known character from this era. Affectionately known as 'the crab woman', she was a regular sight selling crabs from the basket that was transported around town inside a pram. Fishwives were well known for being tough women who had a turn of phrase that could make a miner blush. This photograph dates from 1950 and was taken on Moorgate Street. It is no longer on the map as the street was cleared in the mid 1950s and Mariner's Square now stands here. Moorgate Street had some 40 two storey back to back houses that were built in the 1820s and originally provided comfortable accommodation for the working classes. However, there were many families who had large numbers living in the houses and overcrowding meant that conditions became unpleasant.

Below: As the heavier industries declined and focus shifted to other forms of manufacture and employment, the communications field began to open up after the second world war. During the dark days of the early 1940s, when the world as we knew it began to change forever, one benefit to come from the evil of war was that of technological advancement. Science became important in our everyday lives and was not just for boffins in white coats poring over equations and handling test tubes. The expertise developed out of necessity in fields such as radio, telephone, film and electronics helped inspire the advancement of some established firms and the founding and development of others. This largely female workforce was employed by Ericsson's on Hylton Road, manufacturing telephone exchange equipment. In 1950 few of the working classes had their own phones, but that would change as the decade progressed. Communications had to become faster and more reliable and this company was one of the leading names of the era. Founded by Lars Ericsson in 1876, it has continued to rank prominently to this day. As the women carefully attended to the components on which they were working, they listened to 'Workers' Playtime' on the tannoy, chuckling at the humour of the likes of Ken Platt and his 'I won't take me coat off, I'm not stopping'.

Above: These boys, astride bright Post Office red motorbikes, were ready for the off in 1950 as they prepared to take their telegrams across the region, mainly to those who did not have their own telephones. Important news that could not wait for the letter post was relayed in this way by lads known as telegraph boys. Three of the riders in this group had yet to pass their driving tests, which seems a little bizarre. The telegram was part of our communications culture for well over a century. William Cooke and Charles Wheatstone devised the electric telegraph system in the 1830s and in 1845 the first telegraph service in Britain was established. The actual messages were known as telegrams from the mid 1850s. By the start of the first world war, some 82 million were sent annually. One famous one helped catch the murderer Dr Crippen when he was attempting to escape to Canada in 1910, having left the dismembered corpse of his wife behind in a basement. However, during the 1914-18 War, people developed a fear of the telegram as the sight of a delivery boy on the street invariably meant that there was bad news of a loved one missing in action. Today, with mobile phones and the internet at everyone's fingertips, the telegraph boys are now just an interesting bit of history.

Above right: Coalmining was once part of our lifeblood. Along with the shipyards, the pits provided steady employment for most of their history. Even in November 1979, there seemed to be a future for men such as these. They were among the 938 men employed at Boldon Colliery and were able to celebrate a production record of over 10,000 tons. There were still 34,000 miners in jobs across the north east and they set a productivity record of over 2 tons per man per shift. The area's 28 pits mined 320,520 tons, more than they had for over four years.

Demand from the power stations had increased and a steady supply of coal was needed. No wonder that this band of tired, grimy, but happy men gave themselves a pat on the back. Yet, change was on the horizon and it would come at breakneck speed.

No, this is not the start of the Great North Run, but some of those we can see are moving at a pace good enough for an Olympic sprinter, never mind a half marathon athlete. The reason for their charge out of the gates at Sunderland Shipbuilders is that this was the beginning of the annual shipyard fortnight. This holiday period had become a tradition and one that was echoed up and down the country in different industries, as in the Wakes Weeks when millworkers took their break. In 1979, many of these workers pictured here would have been off to Benidorm or somewhere similar on a package tour. The holiday industry had changed dramatically over the previous 20 years. Where once they would have been happy with a caravan at Scarborough, a boarding house at Whitby or just days out at Roker, there were now new horizons to be enjoyed. Have fun while you can, seemed to be the message. Even the most optimistic knew that shipbuilding in the area was in great decline. Even internationally famous names such as Doxford's had felt the pinch. It united with JL Thompson and Laing's in 1961, leading to the creation of the company we see here in 1972.

H Nordstrom and Son
The Wooden Wonders

Nordstroms is a thriving timber merchant, purpose made joinery manufacturer and Kitchen and DIY Centre. With twenty employees it can boast over fifty four years trading experience, and it still firmly remains a family run business. Nordstroms can be proud to say that it has supplied timber and joinery items to such places as, The Stadium of Light, Seaham Hall and Beamish to name but a few.

It started in 1953 when founder Herman Nordstrom opened a small building supplies business in Nile Street. Five years later he was joined by his son Alan. As the years and the business progressed, the need grew to move to larger premises. In 1972 Nordstroms moved to its present site in Hendon Road. The new premises were the old Glaholm & Robson rope works; again, as each year went by they increased and developed the building and premises further enabling the firm to thrive and increase capacity and to diversify into other areas of design, manufacturing and product choice.

During the 1980s DIY boom, the firm extended further to provide a large kitchen and door showroom. This combined with its staff expertise now supplies many products ranging from plywood and timber, doors and decking, stairs and skirtings to worktops and even a kitchen sink!

Company founder Herman Nordstrom worked until the age of 86, retiring in 1995. Sadly he would only live for another six weeks after retirement. The following year Alan's son David and daughter Lynne joined the family firm. However, Alan is still very much 'hands-on' and takes any opportunity to work at the bench in the joiners' shop, where he admits he is happiest!

Today the business continues to go from strength to strength, and it is now the largest independent timber merchant in the city. It is still run by Alan, his family and loyal team of staff with a combined service history of more than 280 years; providing a personal, professional and efficient service to all customers, as well as a first class delivery service using the company's own liveried vehicles.

Above: Alan and Herman Nordstrom behind the trade desk in the early years. *Below left:* An early photograph of the company premises when under the ownership of Glaholm & Robson, Ltd. Notice the two entrances, at the time of this photograph both men and women had their own entrance to work. *Below:* Part of the Nordstrom fleet, 2007.

Sunderland High School - Continuity and Change

Sunderland High School, situated in the Ashbrooke Conservation area, is one of the oldest independent schools in the city. Throughout the school its staff aim to establish the foundations for lifelong learning. On those firm foundations it builds an enriched school experience which assists all its pupils to take full advantage of all of their talents. Many generations of former pupils are now able to look back on their schooldays in Sunderland and reflect in adulthood on just how fortunate they have been.

In its present form the school was founded only in 1992 from the merger of Sunderland Church High School and Tonstall House, in consequence the school's real history stretches back well over a century and to the days of Queen Victoria.

Its foundation in 1884 owes much to the Venerable Archdeacon R. Long. On his appointment as Rector of Bishopwearmouth Church in 1883, he expressed surprise at the absence of a High School for Girls in a town of the size and standing of Sunderland. He was clearly a man of action as by December of that year he had established that a possible way to remedy this situation was to seek assistance from the newly formed Church Schools Company. Having gained the support, in principle, of local churchmen a committee was formed and a public meeting, chaired by the Bishop of Durham, secured the support of the mayor and leading townsfolk. By April 1884 Sunderland High School for Girls had opened at numbers 10-11 Park Terrace (now Toward Road) with 16 full time pupils. Miss M. Gilliat was appointed as Headmistress. So popular was the new venture that within two years there were 110 pupils and larger premises were urgently needed.

With efficiency equal to that which marked the school's origins, land to the east of Nicholson House was purchased, plans drawn up, the foundation stone laid in February 1887 and staff and pupils moved in to a purpose built school, designed to accommodate 300 pupils, in February 1888. This building is still pivotal to the school, but to meet changing demands and increasing numbers school property has been developed on both sides of Mowbray Road. Sunderland High School has been fortunate in its ten Headteachers each of whom who would oversee major educational developments, not least some challenging building projects.

Top: Miss M. Gilliat, the School's first Headmistress. **Left:** *The original premises of 10-11 Park Terrace.* **Below:** *The purpose built school designed to accommodate 300 pupils, completed in February 1888.*

Miss E. M. Ironside was the longest serving Headmistress. Building on the work of her predecessors she more than anyone was responsible for creating the overarching ethos of the school. Arriving in 1905, she quickly pressed for improved laboratory space, some new pianos, the introduction of swimming and the active participation in practical charitable work. The school was already generous in support of good causes but Miss Ironside wanted pupils to recognise that to work for a cause was as important as giving money. Under Miss Ironside the number of pupils on roll increased steadily. Until 1915 pupils from the Preparatory Department to the Sixth Form were catered for in Main School. In that year, School House was opened in Gray Road to house the Preparatory School, a domestic science room, facilities for music and accommodation for weekly boarders and some members of staff. Miss Ironside was committed to a programme of Physical Education and Games. Early in her career as Head she played hockey with pupils and staff. In the 1920s the school excelled in netball and rounders which could be played in the school yard. Whilst good progress was being made in hockey it had been difficult to find suitable pitches on which to play matches. In 1928 three acres of land at the top of Strawberry Bank were bought and the High School now had its playing fields and later a pavilion. Before her retirement and to mark the school's 50th Anniversary Miss Ironside pressed for and was successful in raising funds for a gymnasium at Mowbray Road.

The war years of 1939 to 1945 brought a temporary halt to both the expansion of pupil numbers and of building plans. Miss N. Horobin, who had succeeded Miss Ironside in 1938, the year before the outbreak of the Second World War, had to face a dramatic fall in roll on the first day of Autumn Term 1939. Out of the 250 girls expected to return to school at the beginning of September only 75 were present. Some had been sent to boarding schools, others were sent to the country by their parents away from the expected dangers of a German bombing campaign. Even though there were 123 girls by the end of term, the school was operating at half strength and staffing had to be reduced.

*Top: Sunderland Girls High School, 1906. **Above left:** Hendon Hill. **Below:** A late production of the Pirates of Penzance, pictured centre is Kate Adie O.B.E former BBC Chief News Correspondent.*

By 1945, however, with victory assured in the terrible conflict which had convulsed the world, Sunderland and the High School were both looking to the future. There were 300 pupils on the school roll and additional space was urgently needed. Hendon Hill was bought in 1946. The house was to be taken over by the Preparatory School and provided an ideal setting. The extensive grounds were to be developed to provide large playing fields with facilities for hockey, rounders, tennis and athletics, and all of this was in easy walking distance of Mowbray Road. In 1947 Miss Horobin left Sunderland to become Headmistress of Roedean public school.

It was Miss C. M. Johnson's first task to oversee the development of and manage the problems of the transition to Hendon Hill, which would be officially opened in July 1950.

Miss Johnson applied to the Church Schools Company council for funding for two new laboratories to improve the delivery of the science curriculum. The existing laboratory was situated on the ground floor of Main School and Miss Johnson took the opportunity of using this space to improve Library provision. Before she left Sunderland in 1957 Miss Johnson felt the name of the school should be changed to Sunderland Church High

School to commemorate its foundation and to reflect the continuing underlying ethos of the school.

Miss J. L. Wisbach was Headmistress from 1957 to 1980. In 1958 a new Home Economics Centre was built next to the gymnasium. Increasing Sixth Form numbers necessitated a building to house the Lower Sixth and provided a much needed teaching area. With more girls opting for science at O and A Level GCE a third laboratory was needed. The Physics Lab was built above an extended Home Economics block. Hendon Hill, too, was extended by the addition of a new dining hall in 1964 which served both schools. Older Sunderland residents may remember the daily 'crocodile' of pupils as they made their way along Ryhope Road to Hendon Hill at lunchtime; a practice which was to continue until 1993. In 1970 The Norma Wilkinson Hall was built in memory of this former member of staff, with the financial support of her husband.

At the opening of the school, Archdeacon Long had rightly stated that the school had been given a building

Top: A girls hockey match at the Strawberry Bank Field.
Above: Boys and girls together on a new playing pitch.
Left: Baroness Platt of Writtle officially opens the Centenary Building in 1987.

and a site that was suitable for extension. However, by the early 1980s the limit had been reached. On her appointment as Head in 1980 Mrs M. Thrush had a vision of a two form entry school. This led to the creation of a Nursery at Hendon Hill and the use of temporary classrooms for the two oldest junior classes. At Main School the top floor was transformed. Attic space was made usable by the creation of dormer windows. The result was an enlarged and airy Art Room and two new classrooms. In the school's centenary year the Church Schools Company committed itself to the provision of a new building to update the provision for Science, Music and to provide additional classrooms.

In 1987 the school celebrated its centenary in the knowledge that its founders' expectations had been fact exceeded and that it could embark on its second century with confidence and optimism in the future.

From the late 1980s until the present the school has undergone a period of radical change and the result is a school prepared for the demands of the twenty-first century. As boys' independent schools opened their doors to girls in the Sixth Form Mrs. Thrush matched that trend and offered places to boys in 1988. This proved a highly successful venture necessitating the building of a new room for an enlarged year group. Sixth Form numbers increased, not only allowing for a broadening of the A Level curriculum but also proving that co-education could be of benefit to the whole school. The Church Schools Company had been founded to further the secondary education of girls, and Sunderland Church High School now became the first of their schools to become fully co-educational. In 1992 the Company agreed a merger with the Trustees and Governors of Tonstall School, a long-established boys' day school. A new school resulted which reverted to the name of Sunderland High School. A major programme began at Hendon Hill to build Tonstall House which provided for a new Junior School and a sports hall for the whole school. In 1994 Tonstall House was officially opened By HRH the Princess Royal.

In 1993 Miss C. M. Rendle-Short was appointed as Headteacher. As university buildings became vacant it

Left and inset: Princess Anne, Lady Jane Prior, Ms Charlotte Rendle-Short and Mrs Ann Yoshida pictured at the opening of Tonstall House (pictured inset), May 1994. Top: A music trip to Salzburg in 2003. Below: National guitar competition winner Adam Cooper pictured with Brian May from Queen, Jimmy Page from Led Zepplin and Dan Hawkins from The Darkness.

was possible to acquire Carlton House as a separate Sixth Form Centre in 1996. The new Junior School rapidly attracted pupils and Miss Rendle-Short took the decision to promote a three form entry Senior School. Clifton Hall was purchased and was transformed from a university hall of residence and administration block to provide six large teaching rooms on the first floor. The Drama Studio and Music Department remained intact and a multi media resources room was provided for Years 7 and 8 as well as a conference room.

Dr Angela Slater, the present Head, was appointed in 1998. Clifton Hall was opened in her first term. One might expect that the school would be ready for a period of consolidation but growth has continued. One of the most prestigious buildings in Ashbrooke - Langham

Tower- opened in September 2005 is now providing an inspiring environment for learning.

Buildings alone, however, do not make a school. The founders of Sunderland High School could not have envisaged the growth, the broad curriculum or the changes in teaching methods which would characterise the school in the twenty-first century.

Top, both pages: Sunderland High School, photographed in 2005. *Left:* The School's 2007 production of Forbidden Planet. *Left inset:* Students camping as part of their Duke of Edinburgh Award Scheme, 2007. *Above:* Langham Tower.

Steel products are available in both galvanised and polyester powder coated finishes

Timber products (apart from panels and trellis which are dipped) are all pressure impregnated to current British Standards.

All concrete fencing products are wet-cast for a superior finish and reinforced with steel rods for strength. Willowcrete is able to undertake any type of fencing contract ranging from the smallest repair to the installation of whole-site perimeter fencing.

The company has many years of experience, and the expertise to offer advice, design input and site surveys together with a quick response.

Having the necessary tools, plant, and skilled workforce Willowcrete is able to carry out fencing works which meet all customer requirements. This has given the firm an enviable reputation in the industry where it is known for quality and service. Many of its customers have used its services time and again.

Concrete and fencing are however not the only strings to Willowcrete's bow. The company is also able to produce steel

Left: A view inside Willowcrete Concrete, 1963. **Above:** *James and Douglas Broomfield outside the company office, 1960.* **Right:** *Deptford Terrace in the 1960s. Willowcrete were situated top right (in front of the gas holder).*

Despite diversification down the years Willowcrete's concrete products remain central to the business. The company produces pre-cast concrete products for both the fencing and building industries. As a fencing contractor many of its products are fence posts and panels, however, the firm also manufacture a wide range of products such as clothes line posts, lintels, padstones, pier caps, copings, doorsteps, thresholds, sills, balustrades, paving, bollards, path/lawn edging and LocBloc dry walling.

The company is also able to manufacture bespoke items to suit customers' own designs and specifications. Willowcrete has invested in a state-of-the-art concrete mixer which ensures the quality of the concrete produced, and also helps to keep pace with rising demand.

gates and steel fencing of any description in its fully-equipped fabrication shop. It also manufactures a wide range of bespoke steel products, such as bollards and bridges, handrails and window grills. Over the years the firm has undertaken many prestigious contracts, including some of the largest gates in the country, not to mention some of the highest fencing.

All gates and fencing are manufactured to customers' exact requirements, often involving precise site surveys being carried out and fabricating special gates and panels to suit sloping ground conditions and other problematic sites.

At Willowcrete everyone takes pride in the quality derived from being a member of a team of first-class and fully qualified fabricators and welders. This is reflected in the many fencing companies and other consumers who purchase the firm's products time and again.

Sale, manufacture and installation are not the end of Willowcrete's involvement with its clients. The company is able to provide a maintenance and repair service using a team of first class fence erectors. It also has a fully-equipped and mobile welding unit to carry out any repairs to steelwork. Repairs can include damage due to vandalism, motor vehicles, wear and tear etc. Whatever the problem, Willowcrete is able to repair fences quickly and efficiently, with minimal disruption.

In recent years prices have risen due to shortages of steel and timber, and to taxes imposed on aggregates and landfill. Natural aggregates, steel and timber are the main materials

This page: A selection of products manufactured and installed by Willowcrete. Top is a pair of 2.40m high by 16.0m wide double leaf gates at the Port of Tyne, centre right shows a perimeter fence at Seaham Redstar football ground, and pictured right is a pergola fitted for Chester-le-street District Council.

A new steel fabrication shop was opened in 2002 and plans for a new cutting shop to go with it are well-advanced. Future plans involve expansion of the steel fabrication and concrete facility, investment in new technologies and working practices to keep up with increasing demand.

Turnover has increased every year and continues to do so. The company now runs a fleet of 10 liveried vehicles, not including specialist equipment such as a JCB Robot and forklift trucks.

Financially the company is in a strong position and is fortunate enough to have an exceptionally good workforce which is its biggest asset.

used by the firm. Recent shortages of natural resources, cost and environmental implications have encouraged re-cycling wherever possible, and buying from sustainable sources.

As well as supplying corporate clients Willowcrete is also open to the general public for the sale of both fencing and concrete products as well as a whole range of other products such as barbed wire, timber decking, joists, handrails and sand, gravel & cement.

Customers are invited to discuss their requirements with the firm's friendly staff who are always happy to offer practical advice on materials, method, quantities etc. Delivery can be arranged (with crane off-load if required) or goods can be collected from the depot.

The company is one of the few fencing contractors able to manufacture almost anything that a customer can come up with.
Technical superiority stems from having qualified management and staff, including Marine Engineering, in addition to time-served fabricators, a Health & Safety Manager with a national recognised certificate in health and safety (NEBOSH) together with hundreds of years of combined experience shared amongst the staff.

The company is proud of its employees – even if their well-known expertise has occasionally been a double-edged sword. Amongst the major difficulties faced by the company down the years has been the poaching of its staff by other companies seeking to make a name for themselves in the market using transferred knowledge.

Jeff Broomfield however feels only complimented by competitors who copy Willowcrete's designs: 'This shows that our products cannot be made any better. We are honoured to set the standards for others to follow. Meanwhile some employees have spent most of their working lives here and their contribution is greatly appreciated.'

Today, with a workforce of more than 30, Willowcrete offers to supply and erect all types of fencing/gates and pre-cast concrete products, principally supplying the North East of England but also reaching areas throughout the UK. What next? Aspirations now involve trade with the Far East, commencing with a trade mission to China in 2007.

Top: Replica gates fitted at Mere Knolls cemetery to replace gates damaged by a car collision. *Below:* The present Willowcrete fleet, 2007.

Edward Thompson - The business founded on a bet

'**K**elly's eye, number one'. 'Legs eleven'. 'Top of the shop, blind ninety'. There can't be many folk who do not recognise those well-honed phrases beloved of bingo players throughout the land. Almost everyone has played a game of bingo at some time in their lives; many enjoy the game so much that they play as often as possible.

But though millions may have played the game very few players will pause for a moment to ask themselves where their bingo cards have come from.

The answer of course is almost certainly Sunderland, and the firm of Edward Thompson.

The name of the Edward Thompson Group with its headquarters in Sunderland's Richmond Street is well known throughout the United Kingdom, and indeed round world, for its expertise in the gaming industry, in particular bingo and other

forms of game cards. It is appropriate therefore that the company was established in 1867 precisely because Edward Thompson, the company's founder, won a bet at horse racing.

Edward won £60, a considerable amount of money at the time. He added his winnings to his life savings and bought property in Sunderland and set up trade as a Printer and Stationer.

As Edward had no children the business eventually passed to his nephew George Curren. George himself was a bachelor, so the business next passed to his nephews George Edmonds, and John Louis Cronin, the latter entering the business after his return from the trenches in 1918.

John Louis Cronin eventually became sole owner and took an active part in the business until his death in 1980. He had been succeeded as Managing Director in 1956 by Frank Cronin, the middle one of his three sons, who by then had by then taken over the day to day running of the company. Frank had joined the

company in 1953 after his return from National Service in the RAF. His older brother John was a Chartered Accountant, and his younger brother Jim was a Roman Catholic priest who served with the Mill Hill Missions in Africa for many years.

In 1959 Frank found a mounting demand for the 'bingo tickets' which the stationery shop, which was situated in South Street and Walworth Street, was then selling.

At that time the company was buying its stocks from a firm in Ipswich, but such was the demand for the bingo cards the supplier could only let the shop have 3,000 books a month.

As, at that time, the company could sell 10,000 books with ease. Frank decided that the only way to keep his customers happy was to print his own tickets.

But first Frank had to devise a 'combination' This is the most important part of a bingo ticket, as each ticket must have 15 numbers, and a strip of tickets must contain all the numbers 1–90. To avoid lots people winning the same game - bingo players want the whole prize, they don't want to share – the ticket had to be designed so that every ticket was different from every other ticket by at least five numbers, and every strip had to be different from every other strip by 15 numbers. Frank's combination, which is subject to copyright, is still recognised as the finest combination in the trade.

The sheets were cut into strips, each strip containing six cards. Machines then stitched the strips together into book form. The books were packed, labelled and added to the always diminishing piles in the firm's stockroom. The firm's proud boast was 'Order one day and the cards arrive the next!'

From printing bingo cards the firm broadened its scope to make all the equipment that went with playing bingo. They offered a 'bespoke bingo service' covering advice, equipment manufacture, installation and the supply of bingo tickets.

Eventually a new factory was needed to cope with the extra work and of course extra staff too. The company bought premises in Wilson Street, on the Sheepfolds trading estate in 1965.

Top left: George Curren, nephew of Edward Thompson, who was a bachelor and and inherited the business from his uncle. **Left:** Sunderland High Street at the turn of the century. At the far right hand side of the picture, Edward Thompson's premises can be seen. The young boy looking in the window had obviously seen something that caught his eye. **Above:** John Louis Cronin (standing) with his mother, two sisters and brother, Donal in 1919. He took over the business from George Curren, along with his cousin, George Edmonds.

Soon there were no fewer than thirteen Heidelberg 10x15 inch platens and five double crown cylinders, most of them engaged in producing up to 50,000,000 tickets weekly, consuming nearly 50 tons of paper. By now Thompsons had a staff of 300 who enjoyed ideal working conditions that included bonus schemes and piped music.

Such was business that even more space was soon needed, and the first floor of what was to become a three story factory was opened in the next street, Richmond Street, in 1967. Increases in turnover and staff meant the further two floors were built and opened in August 1970. By then the company was employing over 500 staff, and the company boasted the greatest number of Heidleberg printing machines (at that time the most famous printing machine in the world) under one roof in the whole of Europe.

Staff would prove to be remarkably loyal. The company recognises its longest serving staff for their loyalty by presenting them with a Gold Watch for 25 years service. Almost 200 staff have now received their gold watch: twenty staff have also received cash gifts after completing an extraordinary 40 years of working for the Group.

Meanwhile, still in the 1970s a fleet of vans ensured that the bingo tickets were delivered to the bingo clubs on time. The bingo industry was flourishing so much that there would have been riots if a club had run out of tickets. It was the company's boast that no bingo club supplied by Edward Thompson had ever run out of tickets.

In 1976 a new phenomenon was to hit the UK. – Newspaper Bingo. What was now the Edward Thompson Group printed the game cards for the Sheffield Star, the first newspaper in England to play bingo this way.

The national newspapers caught on, and then newspapers all over the world. Some of the newspapers even had a prize of £1,000,000 for the winner of their newspaper game, and the Edward Thompson Group was the company of choice for printing these tickets. The firm was soon exporting its products all over the world, and in 1993 was proud to receive The Queen's Award for Export Achievement.

Further expansion was needed to feed this growing market, and new machinery was required. Frank Cronin invented a new printing system which could print every game card with different

by his sons Phil and Paddy. In 2007 Phil decided to concentrate his energy on his thriving internet gaming site, and Paddy took over the position as Managing Director.

Expansion of the company continued with the delivery in 2007 of a new full colour digital press and wide format ink jet machines which can print posters of up to 60" x 40". A Heidleberg printing press at a cost of £500,000 was also ordered.

The company continues to thrive, despite uncertainty concerning its future home with the local council deciding that the Monkwearmouth site is no longer suitable for industry. However, as the company owns all the land its many premises are built upon.

combinations of numbers. For example the company could supply every man, women and child in the UK with a game card and no two cards would have an identical group of numbers on it – a system which is still in use to this day. Frank was very proud to be named on the worldwide patent as the inventor of the system.

The site of the Domtar Paper Mill at Hendon was purchased to house the new press as well as a factory making recycled papers. The Sunderland Papermill traded for 25 years until unprecedented rises in the cost of fuel led to its closure in 2004. Many of the UK's other papermills would close down in similar circumstances.

The company suffered a family tragedy in 2004 when Frank Cronin's wife, Theresa, died. Frank had taken a step back from the company when she had become ill, and his place was taken

With a little luck and lots of hard work Frank Cronin played the game of business bingo to perfection and claimed his own personal jackpot. Today his successors carry on his tradition with undiminished enthusiasm, having branched out into many collateral activities, not least as a major producer of scratch cards and promotional games.

Now in the 21st century Paddy Cronin is leading the company on to even bigger things, and new markets in search of Edward Thompson's next 'full house'.

Left: *Workers checking bingo tickets in the 1960s.* **Above and below:** *The Edward Thompson premises today, a far cry from the tiny shop on Sunderland High Street at the turn of the century.*

George V Cummins - Making Sparks Fly

George V Cummins Ltd is one of the best-known electrical-contracting firms in the Sunderland area. Company founder, George V Cummins, was born in Byker, Newcastle. During the first world war he was an army despatch rider and after the war came to Sunderland and started work for Brantingham's electrical contractors in Norfolk Street.

Through the 1920s George and his wife lived in a flat above Brantinghams, opposite The Londonderry in High Street West, where their sons George junior and Ron were born, with their youngest son Stan coming along later.

During the 1930s George bought a cottage in Palmer Street, Millfield and later after the second world war moved on to Queen Street in the town centre where his business began to flourish.

During the second world war George worked at James A Joblings 'Pyrex' glassworks as a maintenance electrician. Between shifts however, George carried on doing electrical work on his own to grow the business.

Today the firm has a fleet of vehicles - in the very earliest days the only mode of transport was a pole-barrow pushed by hand to carry tools and equipment. Then bikes came in: often man and apprentice would go to a job with metal conduit lengths fastened to the bicycle - the man on the bike and his apprentice trotting at the side to keep up.

George's three sons started working for their father as soon as they were 14, their first wages were £1 a week. Though there were breaks for National Service for George and Ron, and a stint in the Merchant Navy for Stan, they returned to work for their father. Not that all of them were immediately content with their lot: George junior left to work selling and maintaining vacuum cleaners before he eventually returned to the fold.

A good deal of the firm's early business was conducted in the White Hart pub and Lockharts Cafe where many business associates would meet and share work and tall tales. The company still has a long-standing association with some of these original businesses such as Scraftons builders and Stoddart's plumbers.

Above: Founder George V Cummins and wife Mary. **Left:** *George pictured with family on his wedding day.* **Below:** *George Cummins (back row far right) as an army despatch rider during the first world war.*

In 1957 the firm was incorporated as a limited company, with George senior and his wife as its first two directors. Not long after incorporation George senior retired due to ill health, and his three sons became the firm's directors. At that time the firm's assets included George senior's Morris Oxford car and George junior's own Morris Traveller, whilst Stan had only a bike, and poor Ron had nothing more than Shanks pony. The first company vehicle was soon purchased however, a second-hand Post Office van which Ron used.

Soon the business expanded taking in more employees; the firm moved to new premises with the compulsory purchase of Queen Street to make way for redevelopment in the early 1960s. The new purpose-built premises at 26 Wilson Street North then consisted of a small office area and a large workshop/garage and a store. This now became a suite of offices with workshop and storage – eventually becoming fully computerised with the latest estimating and computer aided design facility, accounts and payroll systems.

Not everything however was new: the firm's original bronze nameplate has followed each move. The company continues its reputation for good workmanship and reliability. Continuity has been important, not least with the firm's employees. Loyal staff tend to stay with it over many years, some leaving and returning, in many cases sons have followed their fathers and brothers into the electrical trade.

George junior's son, the third George V Cummins, joined the business in 1977 after leaving the RAF, and in 1984 on his father's retirement through ill health took over his directorship. On Ron Cummins' retirement in 1988 long-standing employee Mike Stubbs joined the board as a director. Stan Cummins retired in 1990.

George V Cummins Ltd merged with PEC Ltd, owned by Ian Reichard in December 2002. Having outgrown its premises the firm moved to Sedling Road, Wear Industrial Estate, Washington. Mike Stubbs retired in February 2007 when Nigel McCoy and Ron Race were appointed as new directors of the company.

On the retirement of George V Cummins in January 2008, and a management buy-out, the firm will be taken forward with Ian Reichard at the helm with the excellent back up team of associated Directors, Managers, Secretarial Staff, and fully qualified electricians and apprentices to fulfil the continuing success of George V Cummins Ltd.

*Top left: George Jnr, Mary and Ron Cummins pose for the camera outside the company's Palmer Street premises. **Above:** George, Ron and Stan Cummins. **Below:** George Cummins and Ian Reichard in front of the new Sedling Road premises.*

Town Centre Garages (S/land) Ltd.

Town Centre Garage (S/land) Ltd is better known today as T.C.C which is the logo for Town Centre Cars. The Company is now based in Ferryboat Lane just off the A19 opposite the Nissan Factory. T.C.C is the largest independent Motor Retailer in the region. Over a period of more than 30 years the Citroen dealership has acquired an unbeatable reputation for quality and customer satisfaction.

The business began with nothing more than a £2,000 loan and a passion to succeed. Today the company is listed as a North East Top 200 company, whilst still maintaining its original family business values.

The firm opened its doors for business on 4th December 1977. Its founders were brothers Philip and Stephen Smith. Both were born and bred in Sunderland, and both attended Quarry View and Havelock Schools.

With inflation soaring, unemployment on the rise and petrol prices having risen to unprecedented heights, only young optimists would consider staking their futures on a new business in the mid-1970s. Happily Philip and Stephen would be more than equal to the challenges ahead of them.

Starting off with just three staff the new business began its life selling quality used cars from a site in Villiers Street in Sunderland town centre – hence the name of the company.

Previously both the Smith brothers had worked for Mill Garages - Philip selling BMW cars and Stephen selling Volkswagens, Audis and Mercedes-Benz. Before going into the sales side of the business however, both Philip and Stephen had obtained City & Guilds qualifications as motor engineers.

That early training as engineers rather than simply as car salesmen undoubtedly played a major part in the company mindset. The 'fire and forget' attitude of some salesmen would never be a part of Town Centre Cars' philosophy. Customers would not only get a good price and a good deal, they would also be assured that the vehicle they bought would be in good running order and would subsequently be maintained by the very people who had sold it to them.

Responsibility for the business was an equal partnership between Philip and Stephen from day one, though individual responsibilities have changed down the years.

The firm left Villiers Street in 1986 to move to Roker, where the business was based for the following 14 years.

The 1980s was to prove a challenging decade for the two brothers as very high interest rates made it difficult for customers to purchase new cars, whilst the closing of the mines and the ending of shipbuilding in the area made times locally even harder than they were in the rest of the country. But despite those difficulties the Smith brothers persevered, determined that whatever the difficulties that might face them they would not be beaten.

That never say die attitude would eventually be amply rewarded when the economic upturn finally arrived. In October 2000 the firm was able to move from Roker to the present site in Ferryboat Lane next to the A19.

Today Town Centre Cars employs over 50 staff retailing new and used Citroen cars and vans, in addition to providing servicing and MOTs. The firm also supplies Citroen parts to the motor trade throughout North East.

Customers come from all across the North East to buy their vehicles at Town Centre Cars. Those customers are incredibly loyal: some are people who first bought cars from the Smiths when they were still selling used cars in Villiers Street more than thirty years ago.

Though the price of new vehicle has actually gone down over the last decade sales have increased dramatically. Turnover has gradually risen over the years from £300,000 in the early 1980s to six million in the 1990s to over £20 million today.

What has been the business secret behind the company's progress down the decades?

Being ISO 9002 accredited and members of the RMI has no doubt helped.

Having the right people too has been critical. Over the years many staff have helped move the business forward: particularly notable contributions have been made by Ann Charles, Andy Herron, and the late Doreen Rogan, more recently Aidan Brough and Finance Director Chris Sopp.

But perhaps the biggest advantage of all is that of being a dedicated family business: brothers Philip and Stephen Smith have imbued the company they founded with their own personal values – a genuine partnership not just between themselves but between their company and their customers.

*Top left: Stephen Smith and Philip Smith in the Roker Showroom, 1987. **Left:** The Roker premises purchased from Howey's in 1986. **Below:** Town Centre Cars' site in Ferryboat Lane next to the A19, 2007.*

Fred Williamson & Sons Ltd
Painting the Town Red…and Blue and Green…

Specialist wholesale merchants to the decorating trade, Sunderland-based Fred Williamson & Sons Ltd is the largest independent firm of its kind in the North East of England.

The firm's roots go far back in time. In 1874 Frederick Williamson was apprenticed to Robert Airey, a well-known clock and watchmaker in Sunderland. Fred thought that he had found his career but after eighteen months into his apprenticeship, Mr Airey died, leaving the young man without a job. After searching around, doing odd jobs here and there Fred finally found another indenture with John Coates, training to be a Paperhanger and Upholsterer. In those days, this was considered to be one trade.

Fred began trading on his own soon after completing his novitiate and by 1884, he had opened his own wallpaper shop at

*Above: Founder Frederick Williamson senior. **Below and right:** Before (right) and after (below) views of the newly renovated Dundas Street premises, 1923.*

Number 2, Dundas Street, Monkwearmouth: remarkably the firm would continue to trade from there for the next century. Fred worked alongside his wife who, in between raising the couple's six children, helped him in the shop. Two of the six children were sons, Fred and Harry, both of whom later became directors of the firm.

Over the following decade the business grew until 1906 when it had made a sufficient impression on The Wallpaper Manufacturers of Manchester (now Crown Wallcoverings Ltd) that they gave Fred merchant's terms, allowing him to resell their wallpaper to other decorators and retailers.

Frederick Williamson's sons served their apprenticeships as painters and paperhangers. That line of business led the firm forwards until the 1920s, when they decided to concentrate on wholesale supply to the painting trade. In 1929 the firm was incorporated as a Private Limited Company, with the shares being allotted to Fred Williamson and his two sons. The records show that the business maintained a steady but reliable growth until the outbreak of war in 1939, when wallpaper and paint factories were converted to war work. Home decorating was an unnecessary luxury; even distemper and whitening were in short supply.

Despite difficult times within two years of the war ending, the firm had expanded within its premises, taking on a new director, Randle Oliver, who had been with the RAF for four years. He took over the wallpaper sales.

Randle Oliver eventually took over the business in 1961 when the Williamson brothers decided to retire, selling Randle and his wife their shares. The Olivers' two sons, Anthony and Christopher joined the firm in 1971 and 1972 and are now joint Managing Directors.

In the following years the firm grew, with another breakthrough coming in 1981 with the firm's appointment as Regional Distributors of Crown Wallcoverings. For some time, the company had been outgrowing its home at Dundas Street and the directors had been searching the area for more suitable premises. It was in 1984, after exactly one hundred years in Dundas Street, that the firm moved to a new location, a 20,000 sq.ft. warehouse in Roker Avenue, which had previously housed British Ropes.

In that same year, Randle Oliver was appointed National Chairman of the Builders Merchants Federation, followed five years later by his selection as National President of the British Association of Wallcoverings Merchants.

A qualified interior design specialist joined the firm in 1991 to provide further expert advice and complete colour projects for show houses as well as commercial and domestic locations such as hotels, restaurants, pubs and offices. In 1998 a curtain-making department was opened with skilled makers and fitters producing professionally-finished articles from the firms vast range of fabrics.

In the late 1990s it was decided to open a network of Decorator Centres. In addition to the already existing depots in Sunderland, Newcastle and Middlesbrough new ones were opened in Darlington in 1999 and Morpeth and Durham in 2006.

Today with a fleet of lorries making daily deliveries to decorators, retail shops, DIY outlets and local authorities the company's customer base is widening all the time. Representatives call on clients from Berwick on Tweed in the north, Hull in the south and Cumbria in the west.

With a record going back more than 120 years, few firm's today can offer their clients such a wealth of knowledge and experience as Fred Williamson & Sons Ltd.

Top left: The staff of Fred Williamson & Sons in the 1960s. Top right: The company's Morpeth Decorator Centre, opened in 2006. Left: Fred Williamson & Sons Ltd's Roker Avenue head office.

John G Hogg - Caring is Their Concern

There are only two certainties in the world: death and taxes. We might be able to avoid taxes but no one avoids life's last act. During the twentieth century, and now into the twenty-first, much has changed: at the start of the twentieth century, still in the reign of Queen Victoria, huge memorial stones and elaborate funeral arrangements were the order of the day - cremation was virtually unknown. Today cremation is commonplace whilst elaborate monumental masonry is rare.

Yet for all the changes some things remain unalterable: sadness, gratitude for a life well-lived, and the inevitable uncertainty and confusion over what to do next.

The passing of a loved one can present many problems, but with the professional help of an experienced undertaker many of those difficulties can be met and resolved with complete confidence in the outcome.

When Sunderland's John G Hogg Family Funeral Directors were named Funeral Planner of the Year for their dedication, commitment and outstanding service to the community the award was unquestionably a well-earned one. The company was judged regional winner from amongst 2,100 other funeral businesses around the UK.

According to John G Hogg himself "All our staff are dedicated professionals, they have regular training programmes to make sure that the bereaved and their loved ones receive the highest level of our personal and professional service".

John Hogg the founder and owner of John G Hogg Family Funeral Directors began in business for himself on 23rd March 1992. Having worked in the profession since leaving school John now worked on his own, and

Above: *Claire Hogg, John G Hogg senior and John G Hogg junior.* **Below:** *J G Hogg's Fairlane Hearse Limousines.*

which has a very strict code of practice which it abides by to the letter. Being a member of SAIF has huge advantages for the bereaved, guaranteeing that a firm is family owned and not part of a large group.

All of John G Hogg's offices and chapels of rest are designed and decorated to the highest standard. with chapels of rest for all denominations. The firm is keen to stress its commitment to a personal service *"We would never give less, than we would expect for our own family"*.

To demonstrate commitment to the community the firm have recently purchased new Fairlane Hearse Limousines and other vehicles.

The bereaved and the departed may have special ideas and special instructions about how a funeral should take place: 'green' burials; the remains sent up in fireworks, or even turned into diamonds. This family firm is committed to doing its utmost to meet each and every wish, to ensure that the final act in life's drama is conducted not only with due decorum but fully in keeping with clients' ideas and expectations.

would continue to do so for several years, though today the much-expanded firm employs five full-time and seven part-time staff.

As an 'unknown' John had to work hard to build up a reputation in competition with other established local firms. Personalising each funeral with fine attention to detail would be the secret of success, providing a local service for local people and using local suppliers for coffins and other materials wherever possible.

At the outset John worked from premises at 59 Mainsforth Terrace West, in Hendon. In 1996 additional premises were opened at St Luke's Terrace, Pallion Road in Sunderland. Most recently, in 2003 a third set of premises were opened at 138 Allendale Road, Farringdon.

In 2005 the founder's son, a second John Hogg, joined his father after leaving school.

In the first year on his own John senior arranged just 16 funerals. Today the firm carries out more than 350 each year at a cost of over a million pounds.

Despite significant increases in costs over the years however John G Hogg remains highly competitive.

Today the firm is very proud to be a member of SAIF (The Society of Allied & Independent Funeral Directors)

Whatever clients' wishes the firm and its staff are there to help. In an era when many family undertakers have sold out to multi-nationals there remains a very welcome place for the personal touch that comes from a privately run business such as John G Hogg Family Funeral Directors.

Above: A horse drawn funeral for a well known character in Pallion, Sunderland. Below: The company receives their award for regional Funeral Planner of the Year from amongst 2,100 other funeral businesses.

City of Sunderland College
Planning For The Future

Today's City of Sunderland College traces its roots to the post-war years. The forerunners of Wearside College - Monkwearmouth College and West Park College - were established in 1962 when Sunderland Technical College became an institution of higher education, as Sunderland Polytechnic - now the University of Sunderland.

Those newly-created institutions took on the former technical college's craft and technician courses, with Monkwearmouth assuming responsibility for the new service sector courses' grammar school premises at Swan Street.

First in the new centre were business courses, whilst a tower block was created to provide purpose-built premises for food technology, baking, tailoring and nursing. Elsewhere, West Park offered courses in engineering and construction. In 1971, these programmes were transferred to a brand new £1 million centre - Wearside College of Further Education.

An 'ultra modern' new college – now the Tunstall Centre of City of Sunderland College - offered industrial and technical training for 1,800 students. In 1972 it was officially opened by Education Secretary Margaret Thatcher. The two colleges were very different, with male-dominated Wearside specialising in training

for the traditional heavy industries and Monkwearmouth, which had equal numbers of young women and men, developing as a general education college.

During the 1970s Monkwearmouth's substantial growth reflected changes in society: there was a dramatic increase in the number of girls progressing to further education as well as a

trend towards older women returning to education as mature students, many of whom went on to complete their studies at Sunderland Polytechnic. Care courses, nursery nursing, hotel & catering and, increasingly, computing, mirrored the skills needs of local industries and demand from individual students.

The college expanded into various other accommodation and, in 1987, took over the former St Thomas Aquinas School premises, now the college's Hylton Skills Campus.

Top, left to right: *A 1970s view of Wearside College, which was once also City of Sunderland College's Tunstall Centre, the College's Bede Centre, formerly Bede School and Swan Street Centre, formerly Monkwearmouth Grammar School.* ***Above:*** *Margaret Thatcher, then Education Secretary, officially opened Wearside College in 1972.* ***Left:*** *The College's Hylton Skills Campus.*

As the region's traditional industries declined during the 1970s and 1980s there were major changes, with mining courses disappearing and shipbuilding reduced to a fraction of its former prominence. A partnership with the Washington-based Bridge women's initiative helped hundreds of women who would not normally attend college gain confidence and tackle further education and, in some cases, higher education courses.

Monkwearmouth and Wearside Colleges became tertiary colleges in September 1989, and, between them, began to provide most of Sunderland's post-16 public sector education.

Wearside College gained a second base in Durham Road, Sunderland, in the former Bede School, and Monkwearmouth acquired the former Shiney Row School. Wearside was given additional responsibility for A-level courses and some general vocational education for the south of Sunderland. Meanwhile, Monkwearmouth expanded its A-level and general vocational provision in the north and west of the city.

In April 1993 the further education sector ceased to be under local authority control. Both colleges became State-supported independent corporations and began to receive funding direct from central government through the Further Education Funding Council. Despite this shift in status, both colleges retained their close links with the local authority.

Three years later in August 1996 the two colleges came full circle, joined once more in a single institution.

Now, with various centres throughout the city, City of Sunderland College continues to support Wearsiders of all ages. City of Sunderland College has three Centres of Vocational Excellence (CoVEs), serving all of Wearside.

To add a twist to the tale – to serve the sixth form needs of the city, three sixth forms have been set up in partnership with local schools. Bede Sixth Form Academy has been established to serve the sixth form needs of the Sunderland South schools, St Peter's Sixth Form College has been established in partnership with the Sunderland North schools and finally Usworth Sixth Form College has been established to serve the needs of those who live in Washington and surrounding areas. In 2006 this arrangement won the prestigious Learning and Skills Council (LSC) Award for 14 - 19 Collaboration which is part of the Association of Colleges' Beacon Award scheme. This award was in addition to the CLA Award for Creativity in Writing, Art or Design on How to Copy Right! and the award for the basic skills initiative 'Test the City' which was won in the previous year.

Today the future for the City of Sunderland College promises to be every bit as exciting as its past.

Top left and top right: Previously Monkwearmouth College's but now City of Sunderland College's Shiney Row Campus, beside shows this being opened in June 1990 by Neil Kinnock, then Leader of the Opposition. *Below:* The AoC Beacon Awards which were awarded to the City of Sunderland College by The Basic Skills Agency, 2005, The Copyright Licensing Agency Ltd, 2006, and The Learning and Skills Council, 2006.

BIRD'S EYE VIEW

The river traffic on the Wear seemed to be quite busy in the mid 1920s as the craft that we can see made their way towards the bridges. However, this was not mirrored in the level of activity in the shipyards. The region was famous for its shipbuilding and its reputation had grown tremendously during the first decade of the century as the order books filled up. But, within a few years, the industry was on its knees. There had been a demand in the years leading up to World War I for warships and ship repair yards. Then came the steepest slump on record, with heavy job losses and unemployment. By the mid 1920s, the unemployment rate in the shipyards was over four per cent. In Jarrow, the town that became famous in the late 1930s for its march on London, there was one of the highest percentages ever recorded, with 74 out of every 100 men out of work at the height of the depression. This view of the riverside buildings includes Robson's Flour Mill. The company also owned some of the housing around the workplace, where employees rented homes that meant that they were on the doorstep. E.C. Robson and Sons also had a steam mill in Queen Street, off High Street, that was at one time the highest building in the town centre.

In 1899 the Sunderland Corporation and North Eastern Railway Company agreed that a railway bridge would be built over the Wear. A connection was needed between the coalfields around Washington and South Dock. Work on what would eventually be named as Queen Alexandra Bridge was begun in 1906 and completed three years later as a two tier road and rail construction. Its four span structure contained some 52,000 square metres of steelwork. It was built using a temporary cantilever, a revolutionary technique at the time. Initially successful, with 6 million tons of coal being taken across annually, a decline in fuel exports meant that the rail section was soon found to be superfluous to needs and eventually removed. The last goods train ran over it in 1921, but this upper deck was pressed into service again during the second world war when it was used to house a searchlight and anti aircraft battery. The bridge is one of those that owed its existence to the transport revolution of the Victorian railway boom and 20th century road systems. This led to new methods of traversing valleys and waterways, whilst leaving enough space for the traditional river vessels to pass beneath. Named for Edward VII's wife, the opening ceremony was attended by the Earl of Durham, on her behalf. Pictured in c1937, Queen Alexandra Bridge was given Grade II listed status in 1984.

D oxford International Park is now a prestigious 50 hectare site located on the outskirts of Sunderland. It is home to a large amount of high specification office space and, with its cutting edge telecommunication set up, offers much to the corporate and financial worlds of big business. Over 8,000 employees make their way there on a daily basis, following their employment at such companies as Barclays, Nike and T-Mobile. Many of the firms and their products would never have been heard of along St Luke's Road in the early 1930s. Industry in this part of Doxford was much closer to the river than it is in the International

Park of the 21st century. Now, road links are much more important. The Forge and Engineering Works that dominates this aerial shot was a major employer on the south bank of the Wear. Many of those living in the neighbouring side streets were used to hearing the hooter summoning them into work each morning. However, by the time of this photograph, many who grumbled about having to clock on early were glad to be able to clock on at all. Redundancies and short time hours were becoming commonplace as the depression started to bite. The Old Forge Surgery now occupies the site of the former works, close to the Pallion Centre.

It is difficult to appreciate, even in this bird's eye view of the city, that much of it is located on a low range of hills running parallel to the coast. On average, it is around 270 feet above sea level, divided by the River Wear which passes through its centre in a deeply incised valley, part of which is known as the Hylton Gorge. About 70 per cent of the population lives to the south of the river. Of all the towns and cities in the northeast of England, only Newcastle has a larger number of inhabitants. The former shipyard areas along the waterside have been transformed in recent times, with several high profile developments taking place. Sunderland has many famous sons and daughters. That excellent actor, James Bolam, was able to use his regional accent to good purpose as part of TV's 'The Likely Lads' in the mid 1960s, and he found further small screen success in the 1970s with the award winning series 'When the boat comes in'. He is still a regular star of programmes being made today. Sports stars Bob Willis and Raich Carter hail from here, as does the musician Dave Stewart. Perhaps one of the most important influences on our everyday life is down to another native of Sunderland. Joseph Swan, born in Bishopwearmouth in 1828, was the scientist who brought us the light bulb.

ACKNOWLEDGMENTS

The publishers would like to sincerely thank the following for their help and contribution to this publication:

Sunderland Echo

English Heritage

Local Studies Department - Sunderland Library

Sunderland Museum and Winter Garden - Tyne & Wear Museums

Andrew Mitchell

Steve Ainsworth

Seamus Molloy

True North Books Ltd - Book List

Memories of Accrington - 1 903204 05 4

Memories of Barnet - 1 903204 16 X

Memories of Barnsley - 1 900463 11 3

More Memories of Barnsley - 1 903 204 79 8

Golden Years of Barnsley -1 900463 87 3

Memories of Basingstoke - 1 903204 26 7

Memories of Bedford - 1 900463 83 0

More Memories of Bedford - 1 903204 33 X

Golden Years of Birmingham - 1 900463 04 0

Birmingham Memories - 1 903204 45 3

More Birmingham Memories - 1 903204 80 1

Memories of Blackburn - 1 900463 40 7

More Memories of Blackburn - 1 900463 96 2

Memories of Blackpool - 1 900463 21 0

Memories of Bolton - 1 900463 45 8

More Memories of Bolton - 1 900463 13 X

Bolton Memories - 1 903204 37 2

Memories of Bournemouth -1 900463 44 X

Memories of Bradford - 1 900463 00 8

More Memories of Bradford - 1 900463 16 4

More Memories of Bradford II - 1 900463 63 6

Bradford Memories - 1 903204 47 X

More Bradford Memories - 1 903204 92 5

Bradford City Memories - 1 900463 57 1

Memories of Bristol - 1 900463 78 4

More Memories of Bristol - 1 903204 43 7

Memories of Bromley - 1 903204 21 6

Memories of Burnley - 1 900463 95 4

Golden Years of Burnley - 1 900463 67 9

Memories of Bury - 1 900463 90 3

More Memories of Bury - 1 903 204 78 X

Memories of Cambridge - 1 900463 88 1

Memories of Cardiff - 1 900463 14 8

More Memories of Cardiff - 1 903204 73 9

Memories of Carlisle - 1 900463 38 5

Memories of Chelmsford - 1 903204 29 1

Memories of Cheltenham - 1 903204 17 8

Memories of Chester - 1 900463 46 6

More Memories of Chester -1 903204 02 X

Chester Memories - 1 903204 83 6

Memories of Chesterfield -1 900463 61 X

More Memories of Chesterfield - 1 903204 28 3

Memories of Colchester - 1 900463 74 1

Nostalgic Coventry - 1 900463 58 X

Coventry Memories - 1 903204 38 0

Memories of Croydon - 1 900463 19 9

More Memories of Croydon - 1 903204 35 6

Golden Years of Darlington - 1 900463 72 5

Nostalgic Darlington - 1 900463 31 8

Darlington Memories - 1 903204 46 1

Memories of Derby - 1 900463 37 7

More Memories of Derby - 1 903204 20 8

Memories of Dewsbury & Batley - 1 900463 80 6

Memories of Doncaster - 1 900463 36 9

More Memories of Doncaster - 1 903204 75 5

Nostalgic Dudley - 1 900463 03 2

Golden Years of Dudley - 1 903204 60 7

Memories of Edinburgh - 1 900463 33 4

More memories of Edinburgh - 1903204 72 0

Memories of Enfield - 1 903204 14 3

Memories of Exeter - 1 900463 94 6

Memories of Glasgow - 1 900463 68 7

More Memories of Glasgow - 1 903204 44 5

Memories of Gloucester - 1 903204 04 6

Memories of Grimsby - 1 900463 97 0

More Memories of Grimsby - 1 903204 36 4

Memories of Guildford - 1 903204 22 4

Memories of Halifax - 1 900463 05 9

More Memories of Halifax - 1 900463 06 7

Golden Years of Halifax - 1 900463 62 8

Nostalgic Halifax - 1 903204 30 5

Memories of Harrogate - 1 903204 01 1

Memories of Hartlepool - 1 900463 42 3

Memories of High Wycombe - 1 900463 84 9

Memories of Huddersfield - 1 900463 15 6

More Memories of Huddersfield - 1 900463 26 1

Golden Years of Huddersfield - 1 900463 77 6

Nostalgic Huddersfield - 1 903204 19 4

Huddersfield Memories - 1903204 86 0

Huddersfield Town FC - 1 900463 51 2

Memories of Hull - 1 900463 86 5

More Memories of Hull - 1 903204 06 2

Hull Memories - 1 903204 70 4

Memories of Keighley - 1 900463 01 6

True North Books Ltd - Book List

Golden Years of Keighley - 1 900463 92 X
Memories of Kingston - 1 903204 24 0
Memories of Leeds - 1 900463 75 X
More Memories of Leeds - 1 900463 12 1
Golden Years of Leeds - 1 903204 07 0
Leeds Memories - 1 903204 62 3
More Leeds Memories - 1 903204 90 9
Memories of Leicester - 1 900463 08 3
More Memories of Leicester - 1 903204 08 9
Memories of Leigh - 1 903204 27 5
Memories of Lincoln - 1 900463 43 1
Memories of Liverpool - 1 900463 07 5
More Memories of Liverpool - 1 903204 09 7
Liverpool Memories - 1 903204 53 4
More Liverpool Memories - 1 903204 88 7
Memories of Luton - 1 900463 93 8
Memories of Macclesfield - 1 900463 28 8
Memories of Manchester - 1 900463 27 X
More Memories of Manchester - 1 903204 03 8
Manchester Memories - 1 903204 54 2
More Manchester Memories - 1 903204 89 5
Memories of Middlesbrough - 1 900463 56 3
More Memories of Middlesbrough - 1 903204 42 9
Memories of Newbury - 1 900463 79 2
Memories of Newcastle - 1 900463 81 4
More Memories of Newcastle - 1 903204 10 0
Newcastle Memories - 1.903204 71 2
Memories of Newport - 1 900463 59 8
Memories of Northampton - 1 900463 48 2
More Memories of Northampton - 1 903204 34 8
Memories of Norwich - 1 900463 73 3
Memories of Nottingham - 1 900463 91 1
More Memories of Nottingham - 1 903204 11 9
Nottingham Memories - 1 903204 63 1
Bygone Oldham - 1 900463 25 3
Memories of Oldham - 1 900463 76 8
More Memories of Oldham - 1 903204 84 4
Memories of Oxford - 1 900463 54 7
Memories of Peterborough - 1 900463 98 9
Golden Years of Poole - 1 900463 69 5
Memories of Portsmouth - 1 900463 39 3
More Memories of Portsmouth - 1 903204 51 8
Nostalgic Preston - 1 900463 50 4
More Memories of Preston - 1 900463 17 2
Preston Memories - 1 903204 41 0
Memories of Reading - 1 900463 49 0
Memories of Rochdale - 1 900463 60 1

More Memories of Reading - 1 903204 39 9
More Memories of Rochdale - 1 900463 22 9
Memories of Romford - 1 903204 40 2
Memories of Rotherham- 1903204 77 1
Memories of St Albans - 1 903204 23 2
Memories of St Helens - 1 900463 52 0
Memories of Sheffield - 1 900463 20 2
More Memories of Sheffield - 1 900463 32 6
Golden Years of Sheffield - 1 903204 13 5
Sheffield Memories - 1 903204 61 5
More Sheffield Memories - 1 903204 91 7
Memories of Slough - 1 900 463 29 6
Golden Years of Solihull - 1 903204 55 0
Memories of Southampton - 1 900463 34 2
More Memories of Southampton - 1 903204 49 6
Memories of Stockport - 1 900463 55 5
More Memories of Stockport - 1 903204 18 6
Stockport Memories - 1 903204 87 9
Memories of Stockton - 1 900463 41 5
Memories of Stoke-on-Trent - 1 900463 47 4
More Memories of Stoke-on-Trent - 1 903204 12 7
Memories of Stourbridge - 1903204 31 3
Memories of Sunderland - 1 900463 71 7
More Memories of Sunderland - 1 903204 48 8
Sunderland Memories - 1 903 204 95 X
Memories of Swindon - 1 903204 00 3
Memories of Uxbridge - 1 900463 64 4
Memories of Wakefield - 1 900463 65 2
More Memories of Wakefield - 1 900463 89 X
Nostalgic Walsall - 1 900463 18 0
Golden Years of Walsall - 1 903204 56 9
More Memories of Warrington - 1 900463 02 4
Warrington Memories - 1 903204 85 2
Memories of Watford - 1 900463 24 5
Golden Years of West Bromwich - 1 900463 99 7
Memories of Wigan - 1 900463 85 7
Golden Years of Wigan - 1 900463 82 2
More Memories of Wigan - 1 903204 82 8
Nostalgic Wirral - 1 903204 15 1
Wirral Memories - 1 903204 747
Memories of Woking - 1 903204 32 1
Nostalgic Wolverhampton - 1 900463 53 9
Wolverhampton Memories - 1 903204 50 X
Memories of Worcester - 1 903204 25 9
Memories of Wrexham - 1 900463 23 7
Memories of York - 1 900463 66 0
More Memories of York - 1 903 204 94 1

Available in the Local Interest section of all major bookshops or direct from the publishers - telephone 01422 344344